WHEN G-D ASKS ME

Devorah L. Kalani

WHEN G-D ASKS ME
© 2015 by Devorah L. Kalani

All rights reserved. This work is protected by international copyright. No part of this work may be loaded, stored, manipulated, reproduced in any form or by any means, electronic or mechanical, including photocopying and recording, or by any information, storage and retrieval system without prior written permission from the author.

Cover design by Brian Beardsley
Photography by John Kalani

ISBN 978-0-9967893-8-7

Lo Tira Press
devorahkalani18@yahoo.com
Like us on Facebook: When G-d Asks Me

Printed in the United States of America

CONTENTS:

Chapter 1: Nightmare on Main Street......17
Chapter 2: Bulletproof............................27
Chapter 3: Tel Aviv...............................39
Chapter 4: Shomron..............................49
Chapter 5: BeShalach............................57
Chapter 6: Bed & Breakfast 2 Miles.........69
Chapter 7: Showdown at Midnight..........83
Chapter 8: When You Sleep with Dogs....101
Chapter 9: To Be or Not to Be Jewish.....111
Chapter 10: Mission from G-d.................129
Chapter 11: Translations.......................149
Chapter 12: The Girlfriend....................159
Chapter 13: The Goat Run.....................171
Chapter 14: Lessons Learned and Unlearned...187
Chapter 15: Becoming a Mitzvah............203
Chapter 16: Miracles............................217

Chapter 17: Enough..............................231
Chapter 18: The Rest of 2003.....................241
Glossary...253

Acknowledgments:

This book is dedicated to Sam, my Red Cross Emergency First Responder teacher; Big Tony, who taught me to shoot straight; Coby, the Sheriff who helped train my dog and me; all the First Responders, Search & Rescue peeps, sheriffs, police, firemen, and others who selflessly help their fellow man and who helped train me; Po-poki, who taught me bravery; my husband John, who understood; all the heroic dog handlers in Israel, who try to stop terrorism; and everyone else who helped get me to Israel. I stood there because so many people helped in big and small ways.

This story can only be told because of Ann Dunham's writing class, whose critiques were invaluable. Dave Dunham, fed my brain with fish, while Ann brilliantly encouraged, pushed, prodded and became my writing muse; and of course, the Interrobang writers' group who used enough red ink on my work to sink a small boat.

A special thank you goes to the people of K'far Tapuach who host the dog team and gave me warm memories and pastries. In addition, I must acknowledge the brilliant doctors and nurses in Israel, without whose dedication and talent this book could never have been typed and re-typed.

Of course the most recognition goes to Mike Guzofsky, who even today keeps the dog team going, and has expanded it to the only civilian Search and Rescue team in Israel. Not only did Mike have to deal with me, but throughout our many and varied arguments, we both knew we were on the Jewish side.

And the LORD appeared unto Abram, and said, unto thy seed will I give this land: and there builded he an altar unto the LORD, who appeared unto him.

Genesis 12:7

For all the land which thou seest, to thee will I give it, and to thy seed for ever.

Genesis 13:15

In the same day the LORD made a covenant with Abram, saying, unto thy seed have I given this land, from the river of Egypt unto the great river, the river Euphrates.

Genesis 15:18

But if ye will not drive out the inhabitants of the land from before you; then it shall come to pass, that those which ye let remain of them shall be pricks in your eyes, and thorns in your sides, and shall vex you in the land wherein ye dwell.

Numbers 33:55

Introduction:

In Tanakh, Chapter four of Judges, the Prophetess Devorah, sees in her mind's eye that right now is the time for Barak, Israel's General, to go and defeat the mighty Sisera. Barak has no such vision. He is a practical leader, who looks at the logic of the situation. He analyzes the pros and cons of Devorah's plan. Lacking the steadfast belief in G-d that Devorah has, Barak relies on outward rational appearances, and his military training. Quite frankly, Devorah's plan makes no reasonable sense.

How can the tiny remnant of a Hebrew army, sorely lacking in supplies and chariots, defeat Sisera who has all the latest equipment? Based upon an outward showing, all indications are that Barak and his army will be slaughtered mercilessly. Naturally, Barak refuses to go. He tries to throw it back on the Prophet who is not versed in male war fundamentals, nor the brutality of actual combat. Barak tells Devorah he will go but only if she goes with him.

Devorah gives it back in spades when she tells him that not only will she go to battle, but that "the glory will go to a woman."

Through miraculous events, Sisera's army is equalized with the Israelites when their chariots bog down in the rain. The battle turns into a rout. Sisera runs away and is eventually killed by Yael, a woman from a nearby friendly tribe.

Was Devorah scared to go into battle? I have no idea, but she went anyway. She went because she believed in G-d more than she was afraid. G-d said the time was now for winning the war. Devorah not only delivered the message to Barak, but actually forced him to act in the best interests of Israel, even when he did not totally "believe."

And what is belief? You either believe, or you don't. To the atheist, my story is simply a woman's adventure story, perhaps a feminist story, definitely a story that lacks a clear-cut justification. The believer, however, feels a compulsion to act far beyond basic altruism, and *that* defies explanation.

Chapter 1
Nightmare on Main Street

Nov 21, 2002 – Eleven people are killed and some 50 wounded by a suicide bomber on a No. 20 Egged bus on Mexico Street in the Kiryat Menahem neighborhood of Jerusalem. The bus is filled with passengers, including schoolchildren, traveling toward the center of the city during rush hour. Hamas claims responsibility for the attack. The victims: Hodaya Asraf, 13, of Jerusalem; Marina Bazarski, 46, of Jerusalem; Hadassah (Yelena) Ben-David, 32, of Jerusalem; Sima Novak, 56, of Jerusalem; Kira Perlman, 67, and her grandson Ilan Perlman, 8, of Jerusalem; Yafit Ravivo, 14 of Jerusalem; Ella Sharshevsky, 44, and her son Michael Sharshevsky, 16, of Jerusalem; Mircea Varga, 25, a tourist from Romania; Dikla Zino, 22, of Jerusalem.

Nov 22, 2002 - IDF tracker Sergeant-Major Shigdaf (Shai) Garmai, 30, of Lod, is killed when an Israel Defense Forces Givati Brigade patrol near Tel Qateifa, in the Gaza Strip, came under Palestinian gunfire. Hamas claims responsibility.

www.jewishvirtuallibrary.org

I awake with sweat dripping everywhere, wet pillowcase, wet hair. It takes extreme effort to wake up from this nightmare.

During the winter of 1998-1999, a plague of evil nightmares keeps me from a solid night's sleep. Always the same, I am trapped in some kind of enormous rubble pile where thousands of people lie dead or dying in horrific conditions. Often I wake weeping uncontrollably, palpable sadness bleeding from my veins.

Living on the major earthquake hub of California, and having survived the Northridge earthquake half-mile from the epicenter, I figure logically, realistically, these dreams must portend the "Big One." Recently, my husband John has begun to have similar dreams.

"Are you okay?" John asks.

"Ummm yeah, I had that dream again." John is already up, sitting with a cup of coffee, staring at me, concerned.

"I never heard you scream so bad."

"You heard me scream?"

Yeah, it was scary."

"Seriously? You actually heard me scream?"

"Yes."

"I was trying to scream in my dream and couldn't. Are you saying you heard me? I actually screamed out loud?" I try to process the dream, and the fact my vocal chords work while I sleep. "Was it like a dog? You know how they bark in their sleep? Kind of like soft screaming?"

"No, you were really loud and scary. I never heard anything like it."

"Really? I'm sorry. Wow. Sounds creepy. What'd you do?"

"I didn't know what to do. Sounded like you were possessed or something." John gestures to a cup of coffee made exactly the way I like it.

"Oh thank you," the warm brown liquid coats my slightly dry throat.

"You know, I've been thinking, we should join a Search and Rescue team." John begins to explain how he has been searching on the Internet through EarthLink, something about a sheriff's team that civilians can join. "I think these dreams mean we have to do something about this. We must prepare to help people. It probably means we are going to have a horrible disaster or something. I think we need to learn about rubble piles and how to rescue people."

My right eyebrow raises, àla Mr. Spock. My feeble arguments are no match for his determination. We both know doing something, anything, is better than sitting around waiting for this premonition to happen. Thus begins our journey into the world of Search and Rescue.

The next weekend, we meet with Los Angeles Search Dog Team, which is a combination of sheriffs, volunteer sheriffs, deputy sheriffs and some civilians, but the civilian members dress in outfits similar to sheriffs with patches embroidered LASD. We both think LASD means Los Angeles Sheriff's Department. It takes us about six months to realize these patches saying LASD actually mean Los Angeles Search Dogs, not Los Angeles Sheriff's Department.

A couple of the team members are morons when it comes to any kind of survival situation. Not only do I not really want a dog, but I do not trust some of those members. In my opinion, the wanna-be-cops are dumber than Brownie Girl Scouts, even about basic camping, let alone survival. The law enforcement members are cool, calm, and collected; but the few... Oh those few. Without naming names, why do stupid people get into positions of power, then wield and hang on to power for dear life? One of the members, I suspect is an axe murderer. My husband wants to join the team. I refuse.

Quite often, young police explorers join the trainings to act as "victims" hiding in the woods, forests, or deserts, for the dogs to track. The stupid leaders stick females alone in deserted areas. Anyone with eyes can see drug dealers riding bicycles exactly where we enter.

Instantly, I make no friends with these "leaders," because as a plebe, a woman, a beginner, one is not supposed to question their almighty wisdom. When I demand the girls not only have a radio, but that they be hid in pairs, it further cements in their tiny brains that I am an enemy. If the moron and the axe murderer did not have it in for me before, they sure do now.

In my mind, there has to be more than one search team in California. I began to research "Search and Rescue" on the Internet. I find another Search and Rescue team. The problem is, the LASD moron and axe murderer belong to that team also.

The thing about the other Search and Rescue teams that I appreciate is they never pretend to be cops or sheriffs. At least that is honest. During the next five years we work with Search and Rescue, Los Angeles Search Dogs, even the axe murderer,[1] as well as many other teams across the United States.

Most K-9 Search and Rescue people enjoy dogs and the great outdoors. It is a fun and interesting avocation for them. To John and me, it becomes a quest. We both had dreams, actually nightmares, that point us in this direction.

---

[1] *There is no proof an axe murderer or moron were ever members of Los Angeles Search Dogs. This is only a feeling I have about two members based on their overwhelming nastiness towards me.

We know we have no time to spare. We have no real timeline of when this big disaster is going to happen, but we know it will. We aren't even sure what kind of disaster it will be. We have many discussions of what it could possibly be. The word "bomb" is mentioned, and almost as quickly dismissed as too incredible. "Earthquake" is the only logical conclusion.

My husband and I are deadly serious in learning as much as we can, as quickly as possible. The rest of the Search and Rescue members, to us, seem lackadaisical. We had both seen what is to come, and know the urgency. We hope we can get prepared in time. Others don't understand our intensity, and of course, we never mention the dream visions.

Search and Rescue is like a wormhole. The more you learn, the more you realize how much more you need to learn. Most SAR teams in California are wilderness, some of which is applicable to Urban Search and Rescue, but Urban is a whole 'nother ballgame. Fire departments usually handle Urban Search and Rescue. Urban is the direction we will have to go, but how?

In California, fire departments take care of Urban SAR or USAR, and they are unionized. This means pay, more pay, overtime pay, bonus pay, and—did I mention it is a paying gig? They do not look kindly on some civilian usurping their money. This is why most SAR civilians in California are wilderness.

A good man-tracking dog can track anywhere, dirt or concrete; but what do you do if you are in wilderness and end up in the city or vice versa? We know the "incident" will be Urban, but we still need to train, so we join the local Search and Rescue team, and nationwide NASAR. We continue to troll the Internet for any Urban SAR opportunity.

We go to conferences and workshops. We ride helicopters, learn to follow track, use a compass with a map, find direction, find or make water, set up a pack with gear (their list), do earthquake simulation, and travel the state training or being the designated "victim" for others' dogs to find. We do not have a dog, but the teams welcome us because we are their "victims."

Later, when we get a Harrier hound dog, we are still welcome, only not as warmly. That is because now, we are direct competition for any call out.

Once we start training for Search and Rescue, we no longer have those horrible nightmares.

One early morning, John leaves for work and I am lazily sleeping in. The phone rings. I roll over and casually pick up my cell phone, flip it open, pull up the antennae to hear John's voice. He frantically says, "Turn on the TV!"

"Why?"

"A plane flew into the World Trade Center."

"What? What's that?"

"A skyscraper in New York."

I am not sure if I say goodbye or what, but the next hours are spent in front of a TV watching 9/11 unfold. Even before the towers come down, I know all those firemen will die. Not premonition, but this time, from the trainings we've been attending.

Oh my G-d, why are they setting up base camp at the base of the incident? That's so stupid; you never set up command post where it can be affected by the incident. In California it is a rule, the ten block rule. All command posts must be set up a minimum of ten blocks from the incident. *I got a bad feeling about this.*

Then it happens, the tower falls on the command post. They lose all their leaders! From all the Search and Rescue training, I know they have no leaders. There is nobody to answer the rookie's radios as they sprint up 100 plus flights of stairs. There is nobody to tell the junior firemen to pull out of the second tower.

* * *

By July 2002, we have acquired a hound and continue our training in Search and Rescue. We also find ourselves part of an emergency first responder class for The Red Cross. This class lasts about nine months. Once completed, we are qualified Emergency Medical Technicians in twenty-two states. California is not one of them.

There is a variety of people who take this class for a variety of reasons. Nine-eleven has affected people in different ways. Wanting to help is one of the ways some people deal with America's national post-traumatic stress. The class is made up of all kinds of people. In my class, there is a leftover hippie from the 1960s, who, in trying to detox his body from the drugs of the sixties, is now a vegan. We do not get along.

"Who cares what happens in Israel. It doesn't affect us here," Hippie Vegan says.

"You better start caring. As goes Israel, so goes the world," I say.

"I don't care. They should just stay on their side of the world. It is not my business, and I don't care," Hippie Vegan says.

Okay, Hippie Vegan doesn't care about anything but himself. He obviously doesn't believe in G-d, so I can't reason with him on that. "The main reason you need to start caring is because, if we don't stop them over there, they will be right here, in America," I say.

"That'll never happen," Hippie Vegan says, smirking smugly.

"Didn't you learn anything from 9/11?" I ask. "When they finish with the Saturday people, they will be right here after the Sunday people. Muslims are patient. They are smart. And, they will be right here if Israel doesn't stop them."

"That's just not going to happen," Hippie Vegan says, waving a skinny suntanned arm.

Sam, our Vietnam combat-medic teacher, calls us in to begin class. My husband wisely drags me away from being anywhere in Hippie Vegan's vicinity for the rest of the day. We have both devolved into the second grader's arguments of "Yes, it is," and "No, it isn't." I glare at Hippie Vegan every chance I get.

The next week is July Fourth 2002. At LAX, a Muslim terrorist walks up to the El Al ticket counter and shoots two people dead. Terrorism arrives on our shores without fanfare, other than two dead Jews. An Israeli security guard is able to shoot the terrorist dead before he can kill more people.

During the next class, Hippie Vegan comes up to me. I fully expect some smart-mouth garbage or anti-gun lecture from him. Instead, he apologizes to me for his simplistic viewpoint.
I am in shock at his admission of being wrong in his assessment of the world. I am not at all happy to be able to say, "Told ya so." Instead, I remain quiet.

Chapter 2
Bulletproof

Nov 28, 2002 - Noy and Dvir Anter, aged 12 and 14, of Ariel, and Albert (Avraham) de Havila, 60, of Ra'anana are killed along with 10 Kenyans when a car bomb exploded in the lobby of the Israeli-owned beachfront Paradise Hotel, frequented almost exclusively by Israeli tourists, near Mombasa in Kenya; 21 Israelis are among the 80 wounded. Osama bin Laden's Al-Qaeda claims responsibility for the attack, as well as for the simultaneous attempt to down an Arkia plane.

Nov 28, 2002 - Haim Amar, 56; Ehud (Yehuda) Avitan, 54; Mordechai Avraham, 44; Ya'acov Lary, 35; and David Peretz, 48 - all of Beit She'an; and Shaul Zilberstein, 36, of Upper Nazareth, are killed and about 40 wounded when two terrorists open fire and throw grenades at the Likud polling station in Beit She'an, near the central bus station, where party members are casting their votes in the Likud primary. The Fatah al-Aqsa Martyrs Brigades claims responsibility for the attack.

www.jewishvirtuallibrary.org

My husband gives a slight nervous chuckle. He is obliging me, doing things he thinks I like. You know—like looking at lipsticks in Macy's.

We discuss all the nutty people, who, after 9/11 became instantly patriotic, hanging flags all over their cars—as if those very same flags will protect them from bombs and bullets.

I pick up a pretty pink color in a gold tube of L'Oréal, Chanel, or some other doo-dad named goop for women to smear on their lips. Makeup companies have long ago convinced women that they can't be desirable without some unnatural color painted on their faces. Cosmetics lay in neat rows behind glass and chrome counters with young unlined women, dressed stylishly in black, acting as gatekeepers to all that glory. It is only the lipsticks that are sitting on the counter untended, available for all to twist; first up, then down. So, I twist the lipstick up and down—one last reminder of civilization before "the trip."

"Is this lipstick bulletproof?" I laugh.

We share a look, then hand in hand leave the department store. He takes me to dinner, our last unexpected week together.

It is only one week since Mike in Israel called me to make arrangements, and to call his friend in New York who will pay for my ticket. Later, when I am questioned at the airport—"You don't know who bought your ticket?"—it will seem odd. Right now, it seems perfectly reasonable.

I have equipment and supplies for months in the unknown of Israel's Wild West Bank or Shomron as locals call it. I keep having dreams of being in Star Trek and going to some outpost in deep outer space, with Klingons all around. I have prepped and packed even the dog. The problem is the dog.

I carefully froze water in his no spill bowl so that he can lick it as it slowly melts during the airplane flight. I have sleeping pills for the dog in case he gets too crazy, even though Dr. Dammit Janet highly recommends against putting him asleep. They are still in my carry-on, just in case. Flashlights, leashes of various lengths, boots, compass, tracking powder, light sticks, hats, socks, vests for the dog, even fifty pounds of dog food, I've managed to get everything into two suitcases and a backpack. In my backpack is his history, his training records, his shot records, letters from Dr. Janet stating the dog's exceptional health, his chip number, a photo of his tattoo, and for me—only a little passport. All the preparations and supplies for the dog, and the airline forgets to arrange heat for the cargo area.

"Can't he just go without heat?" I question the neatly suited navy blue British Airways lady. "You can see he has a towel in his crate. He will probably just snuggle up under his towel."

She stops typing and looks me square in the eye, "It's about minus 200 degrees in the cargo hold."

"Seriously?!" I wasn't sure if she meant Celsius or Fahrenheit but either way it sounds cold. "Is this going to cost me extra money to switch our tickets?"

"No, it's our fault, I can get you on a flight tomorrow." She types madly.

"That won't work, that's the Sabbath! There will be nobody to pick me up. It's an extremely religious place we are going to. I will be stuck in the Tel Aviv airport until Monday, and with a dog!"

"Well then, the soonest we can fit you in is . . . one week. I will be sure to highlight 'Heat the cargo.'" She smiles and passes both tickets to me. The dog's ticket isn't even discounted. His cost the same as a seat in the passenger area.

My husband helps to gather the two suitcases, the dog crate, and the dog, who by now is out of his crate and on a leash, wagging his tail, and flirting with the counter lady. I put on my backpack and we head out to LAX short-term parking.

"We could go for dinner," John suggests. "You know everything happens for a reason."

"Yeah, like what kind of reason?"

"I do not know, but I believe everything happens for a reason."

"Don't tell me the plane is going to crash."

"I didn't say that."

"This is so stressful, I feel like taking one of Dr. Janet's pills." I hold Po-poki's leash while John rearranges the PT Cruiser to hold the crate and suitcases. Po-poki happily jumps up into the safety of his crate and settles down on his towel for the ride home.

* * *

Looking out the window, I wonder, as I often do at these junctures—how did I get here? My mind wanders to that fateful fifth night of Hanukkah at the Third Street Promenade in Santa Monica. John and I were out wandering the streets enjoying the holiday decorations, festivities, and the street musicians. Jugglers vie for attention with magicians, and musicians singing soulful Aretha Franklin renditions of "Santa Baby."

We mosey out of a Jurassic Park fossil and crystal shop and weave between shoppers, one-man-bands, beggars, and skateboarders. Third Street is always fun at night, but the Christmas decorations and colored lights add to the excitement in the air.

Then, John stops dead in his tracks and begins to watch a group of twenty or so men all dressed the same in black suits and white shirts. Their ties swing wildly as they dance around in circles to Klezmer music in front of a Menorah. Occasionally, a red-faced man reaches up and grabs his yarmulke before it falls off his head. Circular hat back in place, his pace picks up with the rest of the men. I indicate I would like to leave.

"Wait, I wanna watch this," John says.

"It's just Hanukkah. Just a bunch of Rabbis," I say, trying to pull him away.

"No, I want to stay."

"Why?"

"It reminds me of Hawai'i. They are dancing and having fun and they're not even drunk," John says. "I like this."

Somehow I know instinctively that women aren't allowed to dance here. Where were the women, their wives, girlfriends, I think. I look around, but do not see any females who appear attached to them. It seems like a solitary male sport, the dancing. And, here I am with my Hawaiian husband who wants to stay and watch them. I try to pull my husband away, but he is glued in awe of the Hanukkah dancing. I look around to see if there is another entertainer close by that I can watch instead of the boring Rabbis.

"Hey, aren't you Jewish?" John asks me, shaking me out of my roving looks in search of better entertainment.

"Well, Yes, but it is just a technicality. It's only because some Rabbis say I am because my mom is Jewish. They are bossy with weird rules, and I don't know if I agree with them. I really don't know much about it.

"I wanna be Jewish."

"What?!" I say.

"No. Really, I like this. I think we should be Jewish."

"I don't think that is a good idea. You are already a minority, now you want to be a double minority? You know, people like Hawaiians. They do not like Jews. I don't think you should do this. It's a bad idea. I'm not really Jewish, it is just some weird idea the Rabbis have. It's only a technicality. Why would you want to be hated? I mean seriously, it is a terrible idea. My grandma even says, 'there is nothing for women in Jewish.'"

Finally I am able to wrestle my husband away from the dancing Rabbis. I hoped he would forget about wanting to be a Jew, but he wouldn't stop. Finally, after a couple of days of my arguments, I agree to "be a Jew."

"One year. I'll be Jewish for one year, then that's it," I say breathing out.

Neither one of us has any idea how to go about "being Jewish" or practicing the religion. So, we pick up the Los Angeles *Jewish Journal*. It has a list of all the synagogues in Los Angeles. They are categorized by Reform, Conservative, Orthodox and something called Reconstruction. We cut out the list and hang it on our refrigerator. I know Reform is the easiest, so we start with them and spend the next year going to every Shul in Los Angeles. During the later months of the year we start to branch out and try a Reconstruction synagogue and even some Conservative ones.

One Shabbat we go to one of the oldest Conservative synagogues in LA. They are beginning their Saturday morning prayers, before service. They are praying in Hebrew! We do not know any prayers, or how to read Hebrew, or anything. I look around and get scared. There aren't even any women in the temple. We decide to leave. But how to gracefully leave when clearly we are the first visitors since, well, maybe since this Shul was built. The men have noticed us! As we are almost out the door, the men stop their praying and say, "Wait come back." That scares us even more. So we run, or walk very fast outside. They give chase, and keep saying, "Stay, stay. Really, we are friendly. We are nice people."

We yell over our shoulders, "We have to go to a bar mitzvah, this is the wrong place." We hurry around the corner, get in our car and quickly drive out of the parking lot. "Whew!" We look at each other. We do not even know anyone who could get bar mitzvahed. We had lied.

"Do you have the list?" John asks. We go to the last of the Reform synagogues on the list, that day. We meet Rabbi Finley and stay with him for a while, taking all his classes on Jewish religion and practices. We like Finley, so we would often do Friday night at one Shul, then spend Saturday with him. His mother even tells us we should try Orthodox, but we still have to get through the list of Conservative temples first. We had gotten pretty scared of Conservative synagogues, when the men chased us saying how they were nice. So, we put off going to any of the Orthodox Shuls.

Of course, since every Rabbi in Los Angeles says the Kabbalah Centre is evil, we know we have to go there. We try numerous times to visit, but it always seems to be shut tight. We wonder what we have to do to get inside. Do you need a reference, or an invitation, or what?

Then one night, after visiting a Conservative temple, precisely as we drive home past the mysterious Kabbalah Centre, the Spanish style doors open at exactly the moment our car passes. Light and singing hit our ears.

"Quick, stop the car!" I say. Magically, a parking space opens directly across the street. We park and run across Robertson Boulevard into the Kabbalah Centre, determined to find out what is inside. They are doing Kiddush, but here everyone participates and has a little tiny cup of wine. Someone hands each of us a sample-sized taste of wine. They push us into the respective men's and women's sections. Curiosity keeps us from rebelling against being separated.

We stay at the Kabbalah Centre for a couple more years. We both continue studying and I even sing for a while with the University of Judaism's choir. My threat of "only one year" has long been forgotten, as the years flip by.

* * *

I look over at John pulling into Louise's restaurant. It is dark and we are miles from LAX and the British Airways fiasco with that minus 200 degrees. We order take out of my favorite, a chopped salad from Louise's Trattoria. We stop at the grocery store and pick up a bottle of wine, French bread for croutons, and then head home.

I space out for the rest of the ride home. I wonder why I have not told my mother about going to Israel. I'm not sure, but I will meet others who also do not tell their mothers. It may be two reasons, one not to worry them, and two, not to be talked out of our missions. I find out later that I am not the only one on a mission.

Chapter 3
Tel Aviv

Dec 12, 2002 – Corporal Keren Ya'akobi, 19, of Hadera and Sergeant Maor Kalfon, 19, of Kiryat Yam are killed while on guard near the Tomb of the Patriarchs in Hebron.

Dec 20, 2002 - Rabbi Yitzhak Arama, 40, of Netzer Hazani in Gush Katif, in the Gaza Strip, is shot and killed on the Kissufim corridor road while driving with his wife and six children to attend a pre-wedding Sabbath celebration in Afula. The Islamic Jihad claims responsibility for the attack.
www.jewishvirtuallibrary.org

After a week of extra goodbyes, it is good to finally get on the airplane, but, not until after I take off my twelve-hole boots. I carefully unlace, then re-lace them. The welfare-to-work TSA screener tries to apologize for having to pat me down, and scan me with her magic wand.

I look her in the eye and say, "I don't know why you are searching me. I am not on the team that does bad things." I indicate with my eyes toward a woman in a hijab walking through with no pat down. My husband kicks me, trying to get me to be quiet.

Ms. TSA looks at me quizzically. "What do you mean?" She doesn't seem to even notice the upholstered woman.

"I'm Jewish. It is the other team that is killing everyone."

"Shhhhhh-sh shhh." John tries to intercede, to get me to stop talking.

Ms. TSA looks at him and then again at me. "Y'all are finished."

With boots laced back up, backpack once more in place, we head toward Departures. I worry out loud about my dog. John reassures me he will be okay, and that the airlines are professionals. He's going on and on about how they transport horses all the time for horse races. I'm watching the waiting area. It seems to be filled with many Orthodox Jews, standing and praying. They are saying some prayer for traveling. I don't know it, but I know of it.

"Looks like we got some angels watching out for us." I point my chin in the direction of thirty or so black hat dudes standing, rocking, and facing east softly reciting prayers. Their colorful wives, sitting, nursing, watching children crawl on the carpet, they occasionally shush noisy ones. They finish praying and a cacophony of cell phones begins—ringing, flipping, talking, or screaming, in one case. We say good bye and I line up with everyone else.

I find myself center seated about midway on the airplane. I am one of the early ones. The thirty or so black hat dudes are getting onto the airplane; then more, and more Orthodox men. I am surrounded by black. My orange Search and Rescue shirt screams embarrassingly that I am most likely Secular, or worse, a "shiska."

From what I can see, I am the only female on a plane full of Rabbis. I try not to put my elbow on the armrest for fear I will touch the black hat Rabbi seated next to me. Even though I am assigned in the middle, where two Rabbis could possibly touch my long sleeved orange shirt, I take the aisle seat. I think, at least this way, there is only one Rabbi I might possibly unkosherize, or offend, or well, I try to make myself invisible. I crunch down in my seat and think maybe I can reach my backpack stowed under the seat in front of me and get my tracking gloves. Maybe if I wear gloves it will help.

I keep my eyes forward. I pull the bill of my hat down, hiding my eyes. I dare not talk to anyone for fear it will look like flirting. After all, these are the guys who have kept Judaism's mores, ethics, laws, commandments, and prayers alive. I am pretty new to this whole Orthodox thing. Even though I am breaking one of the rabbinical rulings about dress by wearing pants, I am still Orthodox. Even if I do not agree with rabbinical rulings on clothing, I still respect those who do. Just because I can't, I really have a huge desire to put my arm on the armrest. We still haven't taken off, and I am fighting the urge to simply plop my arm on the armrest.

"Excuse me." I look up at the sound of a female voice. "Do you mind switching seats with my husband?" the only other woman on the flight asks me. "It's just that they are afraid that..." She tries to gently inform me it is nothing personal, just how they are Orthodox. She starts to explain the rules about men and women.

"No, no, no of course, it is okay. I totally understand. You don't have to explain," I cut off her excuses. "Just show me where you want me to be. It is no problem, really." I follow her to where her husband was seated, and take his seat next to her. I re-stuff my backpack under the new seat. *At least she doesn't have a bunch of screaming toddlers with her.* I settle in for the long flight. "Now I do not have to worry about accidentally using the armrest," I say to her. She smiles and lets me have the armrest the entire flight.

Once we land at the Tel Aviv International Airport, the Rabbis pick a corner and begin to sway and pray again, thankful for a safe flight. I never really could sleep sitting up. Through bloodshot eyes, I see my passport finally stamped, and the girl wishes me "Welcome to Israel." I ask where to pick up animals.

She is confused. "You brought a dog?"

"Yes"

Back and forth: Kelev? Dog? Why? Really? Finally she calls someone, then she points over there. I go over there. I look for the dog crate. It is not coming off the luggage belt. I ask more questions. I wait more. The Rabbis are still praying. I panic. I ask all the baggage handlers. They point in many directions. I go everywhere searching for the dog. No crate, no dog. I am tired, and worried about Po-poki.

"Where is my dog?"

"I do not know. Not here."

"What do you mean you do not know? How do you lose a dog?"

"I guess we lost it."

"What? Oh my G-d! It's not a piece of luggage, it's alive! You can't just lose it! Where is it? It could die without food or water!

"Well, come back tomorrow."

"What! Are you insane? He could be dead by tomorrow! What have you done with my dog?" I have gotten louder and louder in my arguments and pleadings, so much so that the Rabbis look up from their prayers. I do not care. I find my cell phone and call my husband back in California. I am loud and on the verge of hysteria. He is in the middle of the film editing class he is teaching at Columbia College, Hollywood. He tries to calm me down. I get odd glances from the praying Rabbis.

Then, one of the luggage handlers points to my dog crate in the corner. I hang up the phone and run over to the crate calling his name "Po-poki, you okay? Po-poki?" I get to the front of the crate and look in expecting to see a happy hound wanting to get out of his crate and pee. There is nothing in the crate.

"What have you done to my dog? Where is the dog?" On the crate it reads, "Empty London" in purple felt tip marker. "Is Po-poki in London? Why is the crate empty? Is the dog wandering the streets of London?"

Okay, I lost it at this point. So I begin a frantic pacing, talking loud and very loudly. All right, never mind, I am screaming and pacing. "What the fuck have you done with my dog? I am of no use without my dog. I brought the dog. I trained for five years and the dog for two years specifically to help. Now look. I can't help at all, because you lost the dog! He's not a piece of luggage!"

I pull my pony tail, still pacing. Then I look at the wall and decide the wall of the Tel Aviv airport is most likely bombproof, certainly it is shoe proof. So, I kick it. The praying Rabbis give me sideways looks. They hurriedly finish their prayers and leave. I kick the wall. I kick it hard, and very, very hard. I keep kicking the wall, having a frustrated nervous breakdown on the Tel Aviv International airport wall.

I think back on the London layover and the Royal Society for the Prevention of Cruelty to Animals insisting the K-9 leave the airport to go to their facility and be inspected. They insisted the dog be allowed to "play and pee" before continuing on to Israel. I had the British Airways desk call over to the RSPCA and tell them to not let the Harrier off leash because he will run away, following a track somewhere, anywhere, everywhere! I now have visions of the dog happily running wild on the streets and motorways of London.

I kick the wall so much so, that I feel the metal plate in my right boot bend. I wonder if the bent metal plate will hamper my walking. I continue to kick the wall. Visions of me hobbling, as I try to run after the hound with a bent metal plate in my boot course through my mind. I brush the thought aside, and continue to kick the wall.

The manager of British Airways, Israel comes over to me. He shows me a completely different crate. A giant crate, big enough for a small horse, handmade entirely of wood, has my dog in it.

"Why is the dog in this crate?"

"The RSPCA thinks your crate is too small, so they put him in this crate."

"My crate is made for sixty-five pounds. He is only fifty-five pounds."

"They said it is not big enough. They will probably fine the airlines."

I had thought of everything except to leave the information *about* the crate *on* the crate.

"You know, you should not do this to yourself. You can give yourself a heart attack," the British Airways Manager says gently.

"I am sorry." I blush slightly, half smiling sheepishly.

"Is someone picking you up?"

"Yes, they said they would be in a security vehicle from the village."

This kind gentleman then calls my contact person, and helps me with my luggage, crates, and dog out to the curb. I feel like a jerk.

A white truck with flashing lights arrives. I meet Mike and Josh, or as he would later be known Big-Hair Josh, when another Josh shows up. For right now, we drive into the early evening with my dog, Mike, and Josh, out to the West Bank, somewhere.

"How was your flight?" asks Mike, hoping for small talk and politeness.

Instead, I proceeded to tell them about how the airline lost the dog and I freaked out. I finally end the story with, "I must be the only person who arrives in Israel and kicks the Tel Aviv airport wall."

"Maybe we should dump her off in the local Arab village," Mike suggests. They both chuckle.

"Oh no, don't do that," I say, wondering if they are serious.

I think about my grandma's father, all five-foot two-inches of him, chasing a six-foot four-inch, then fiancé—now my grandpa—up and down the streets of San Francisco with an axe. All the while, Great-Grandpa is screaming "He's a Gentile!" I know I have volatile genes, but the thought of being dumped off in a Muslim village is horrifying, even if it is a joke.

I look out the window at the changing sky. I hope they don't think I too, am a Gentile and carry out the Arab village threat. I release a deep breath and settle into the ride toward what will become my home for the next months. An Israeli news station blares Hebrew over the drone of the engine. I glance at my hosts and hope I haven't made a mistake. We drive on as the last remnants of orange fade to a clear starry sky.

Chapter 4
Shomron

Dec 27, 2002 - Four Yeshiva students: Staff-Sergeant Noam Apter, 23, of Shilo; Private Yehuda Bamberger, 20, of Karnei Shomron; Gavriel Hoter, 17, of Alonei Habashan; and Zvi Zieman, 18, of Reut are killed in Otniel, south of Hebron, while working in the Yeshiva kitchen, serving the Shabbat meal to 100 students in the adjacent dining room. The two terrorists from the Islamic Jihad, claims responsibility for the attack, and are killed by IDF forces. Ten others, including six soldiers, are wounded in the attack.

Jan 2, 2003 - The charred body of Massoud Makhluf Alon, 72, from Menahemiya in the Lower Galilee, is found in the northern Jordan Valley in his burned-out car. The Fatah Al-Aqsa Brigades claims responsibility for the murder.

www.jewishvirtuallibrary.org

We arrive at the summit of K'far Tapuach and turn right up the hill. An abandoned bus sits on one side of the road, bus stop on the other. The highway is well lit; turning up the hill we lose the streetlights. Blackness surrounds the security vehicle we are riding in. Gears grind, not so much from the hill as from Mike missing a gear shifting. Josh pulls an Uzi from between the seats and places it in his lap, barrel facing out. Headlights bring the hillside into an eerie moonscape reality.

We reach our turn-off, and are blinded by bright lights aimed specifically at the driver. I say something stupid like, "Maybe they should adjust those lights, somebody could hit something," not realizing they are already "adjusted" specifically to blind any driver approaching the village. Josh and Mike ignore my comments.

We swerve around enormous three-to-four foot concrete blocks placed in such a way that you have to drive a giant "S" before getting to the gate. There are about half a dozen of the giant children's ABC blocks standing guard in the road. I imagine how they would look painted like the kid's toys.

"They blocked the road," Mike says.

I look out the window at the concrete blocks and think the Israelis must take things quite literally. When Americans say "block the road" it could mean a tree fell over the road, or cars are in the road, or any number of things is preventing the use of the road. When Israelis say "block the road," they literally stick big blocks in the road. I wonder if they have a sense of humor.

The two military guards come out of their hut and begin a conversation with Mike. To me it sounds like "blah blah blah cough blah hock-a-loogie blah blah." I listen, hoping to understand. The guards look at me, then in the back at the dog. Mike answers, "blah blah blah cough blah hock-a-loogie blah blah." We pass inspection and are motioned in.

The whole process reminds me of getting on the military base to visit Dad during my childhood. Later, when my husband, who did not grow up in the military visits, he gets somewhat wigged out by all the weapons. Right now, for me, the M-16s and side arms seem somehow comforting.

We drive through a village of identical white stuccoed houses. The streets look silent, empty, and clean in the evening. In the light of day, the cleanliness will be called into question, at least by me. I am summarily dropped off at one of the white houses. Mike tells me I will be sharing it with another woman, Carol.

Josh helps get my suitcases, dog, and my two dog crates into Carol's house. Mike has to help Josh carry the RSPCA mini horse crate inside. A bed is found and a four-inch camp mattress laid on the hard wooden bed frame.

Carol is introduced, and the guys leave me alone with my new roommate. She seems nice enough. She grew up in California, but she continues speaking to me in Hebrew even though I immediately tell her I cannot speak Hebrew.

I feed the dog and change into my scrubs which I use for sleeping. The house is cold, so I have the dog sleep on my legs. With a body temperature of 102, he is welcome warmth.

Po-poki whining to go out, wakes me up. I take him out, feed, and water him. Carol is already gone. After the dog eats, I take him for a walk, being careful to count how many houses I walk down each block. I notice there are no numbers on the houses. The white houses with red clay roofs all look the same. There aren't even landscaping differences. The few smallish trees are planted in the sidewalks which are made of new red brick laid in a herringbone pattern.

I call my husband and apologize for the late hour. I tell him where I am and how things are going, so far.

Mike shows up and takes me to the kitchen-mess hall. He says there will be two formal meals, breakfast and dinner. This is where we will get our assignments for the week. The kitchen will always have coffee, tea, or hot chocolate, and maybe some cookies. There seldom are any cookies. There is what I lovingly refer to as "chocolate grease," an Israeli copy of

Nutella. It looks exactly like chocolate stirred into Crisco, which you can smear onto pita or a cracker. It isn't bad if you are hungry.

"You can remember where the kitchen is, because it is three houses down from the end of the street," Mike says as we leave the house. Carol shows up in the kitchen and begins cleaning the coffee area.

Later, I would realize horribly how he had counted three houses, then the kitchen. I count three, as in the third house.

He shows me the kennels, the store, and introduces me to yet different sentries at the guard shack. He points out a public telephone—it never works. I look around at the rocky terrain. It looks exactly like the deserts just beyond Los Angeles.

"I gotta go to town and get things for Shabbat," Mike says. He then leaves me until dinner.

I wander around, walking Po-poki, and carefully picking up his poop, exactly like I would do in Los Angeles. I put a plastic bag over my hand and arm, grab the hot poop with the plastic-covered hand, and then quickly flip the plastic inside out covering the poop. I tie a knot before I take a breath. It is quick and painless if you hold your breath and work fast. I get weird looks from some of the ladies. I notice poop piles here and there, on the sidewalk, near the sidewalk. Well, nobody is going to say my dog pooped up the village. I sling the poop bag up into the green dumpster sitting at the end of the street. A family of cats scurries away.

Back at Carol's house, I inspect my suitcases and supplies. Mike has offered for me to use their dog food at the kennels. I decide to stick with what I brought until Po-poki gets acclimated, then I will begin a gradual switch to the Israeli brand. Po-poki is happy to simply hang out in my bedroom sleeping. Nice thing about hounds, they like to sleep when they aren't working. For a hound, sleeping is a form of work, so I don't have to worry about entertaining my dog.

I power up my laptop and write in what becomes my journal. As the battery drains, I look for the inverter I bought at China Central. I find the correct adaptor for Israel, and plug in my laptop. I continue to type while waiting for the charger to begin charging the laptop's battery. Instead, the charger begins smoking. I pull it out of the wall, and my laptop dies. I stare at the blackened charger and wonder how I will use my laptop or where I will get a charger.

Wal-Mart is such a rip off, I think to myself. The cheap plastic "inverter" is made no better than those electric room deodorizers. They know it, too. They know nobody will try to take anything back in whatever country they go to, because no other country allows Wal-Marts. So, if you go on a trip, you spend thirty-five dollars on a supposed "inverter" they couldn't care less. They know you can't bring it back.

I decide to go to the kitchen and get a cup of coffee. I put on my black and white urban camo pants and shoes. The dog looks up to see if it means a walk. When he realizes it doesn't mean him, he goes back to sleep on the bed.

I leave the block I am on and walk around the corner to where the kitchen is. Three from the end, I think to myself, they really should put up some kind of sign or something, but then again, probably everyone knows where it is. I carefully count three from the end. I open the door expecting to see the rows of tables and the cart with coffee, and maybe cookies. Instead, I see a woman in a floor-length skirt. She stands quickly, puts her back toward me shielding a baby. I see living room furniture. She says something to me in Hebrew. She freezes, I freeze. Damn, I have opened the front door of a stranger's home. My face turns fifty shades of red, "I am so sorry."

She realizes I speak English, so she switches to English, "Don't shoot! Don't shoot! Don't shoot!"

My eyes widen. I do not even have a gun. Why would she think I am going to shoot, I think. Bewildered, puzzled, confused, embarrassed, horrified I am sure something shows on my face, but what?

"Oh my G-d, I am so sorry, I am looking for the kitchen, I am sorry, I opened your door. I got confused, I am sorry, forgive me. Really I am sorry, sorry. The houses all look... I am sorry." I am pointing and backing out the door.

She points, and then breathes a sigh of relief. I shut the door behind me. Kicking myself, I recount the houses, not the third house, but three from the end.

Finally, I find the kitchen. It is empty of people. I make a cup of instant coffee with cream, no sugar, relieved to be alone in my embarrassment. I think back on Halloween Trick-or-Treating in America and, how as a child, I would get lost because I would look up to marvel at the stars. I must have turned around looking at the stars, but I would end up at the same house twice. The lady of the house would yell at me for being selfish, trying to get extra candy. I didn't do it on purpose, like the lady accused me. I was just so incredibly amazed by the stars I forgot which direction I was going.

Today, this is broad daylight! And, I dunno, somehow by the tone, and the look on the face of the lady with the baby, somehow, this is much more serious.

Chapter 5
BeShalach

Jan 5, 2003 - Twenty-three people: 15 Israelis and 8 foreign nationals are killed and about 120 wounded in a double suicide bombing near the old Central Bus Station in Tel-Aviv. The attack is carried out by two members of the Fatah Al-Aqsa Martyrs Brigades, with the help of the Islamic Jihad. The Israeli victims: Moshe (Maurice) Aharfi, 60, of Tel-Aviv; Mordechai Evioni, 52, of Holon; Andrei Friedman, 30, of Tel-Aviv; Meir Haim, 74, of Azor; Hannah Haimov, 53, of Tel Aviv; Avi Kotzer, 43, of Bat Yam; Ramin Nasibov, 25, of Tel-Aviv; Staff Sergeant Mazal Orkobi, 20, of Azor; Ilanit Peled, 32, of Azor; Viktor Shebayev, 62, of Holon; Boris Tepalshvili, 51, of Yehud; Sapira Shoshana Yulzari-Yaffe, 46, of Bat Yam; Lilya Zibstein, 33, of Haifa; Amiram Zmora, 55, of Holon; Igor Zobokov,

32, of Bt Yam. Foreign workers: Krassimir Mitkov Angelov, 32, of Bulgaria; Steven Arthur Cromwell, 43, of Ghana; Ivan Gaptoniak, 46, of Ukraine; Ion (Nelu) Nicolae, 34, of Romania; Guo Aiping, 47, of China; Li Peizhong, 41, of China; Mihai Sabau, 38, of Romania. Zhang Minmin, 50, of China died of her wounds on January 13.

www.jewishvirtuallibrary.org

Carol tells me her back door doesn't lock properly and how she is worried about terrorists breaking into the house; the house I am currently living in. She shows me the back door. We pile up some junk; some boxes and other stuff in the utility room leading to the back door. I ask her if she has tried to nail it shut. She hasn't because she doesn't have a hammer. I ask if there is a hardware store around. She doesn't know, but thinks perhaps there is one in Ariel, the closest city.

I go outside and stick the biggest rock I can find up against the door. At least it won't be flapping open looking like an easy target.

I then take a shower quickly with water only lukewarm from the solar water heater. I assume the water is not hot because it has been overcast all day. It isn't until later when someone at dinner tells me about a red button you have to push that turns on the actual hot water heater. You must push the red button fifteen minutes to a half-hour before you need the hot water.

I arrive at the kitchen in time to do the candle blessing. Then, I help Mike finish setting the tables and arranging all the salads, challahs, pitas, grape juice, and wine. Some of the Yeshiva students and Big-Hair Josh are smoking and talking. They switch seamlessly from Hebrew to English and back again. Big–Hair Josh makes a cup of coffee, carefully stirring in sugar. He takes a sip, then quickly opens the door and tosses the rest of the mixture out the front door. He throws the Styrofoam cup in the trash.

All of a sudden, everyone runs off to Shabbat services at various Shuls in this tiny village. I don't know where is the Chabad Shul, so I go home and feed the dog. I wait about half an hour until I think services might be over, and then head back to the kitchen.

At the Shabbat table, I meet some of the villagers and, Moshe, whom I am told I will be doing guard duty or "shmira" with, in the coming week, Yocheved and her two daughters, various kids from the neighborhood, and many visiting young adult Yeshiva students. The dining room is open to all who want to share Shabbat. Some people bring a dessert, a wine, or a dish, but if you don't bring anything, that too is totally fine. Some of the younger kids stay for soup and a bit of bread and hummus then leave. Others stay for the entire meal.

Jonathan stays for the whole meal. Everyone sings traditional Shabbat songs as well as patriotic, kabalistic, and nationalistic songs. I am so glad I know almost all the words to the songs. Jonathan sings his favorite ones as loud as he can with full gusto and heart. Yocheved pours me another glass of wine. We look over at Jonathan singing loud enough to annoy the nearby Arab village. Every Shabbat he enters his own contest, to see how many sleepy angels in heaven he can wake.

"If you can't speak Hebrew, how do you know these songs?" Mike demands.

"I used to sing with the University of Judaism's choir, in LA," I say.

"But how do you sing in Hebrew?"

"Easy, you memorize. Many people sing in languages they do not speak. You just memorize. We even sang at the fiftieth anniversary of Israel's founding at some Holocaust Memorial park in LA. A lot of big mucky-mucks, mayors, ambassadors and all were there too."

I think back on the LAPD bomb dogs and how one handler told me they were under strict orders to search the park for bombs, then to get the dogs out of there immediately. When I asked him why, he told me there would be many Holocaust survivors who have trauma associated with German Shepherds. They must make sure the dogs are gone long before the start of the program, he told me.

At dinner, everyone has a great time over white table cloths and candlelight. It's festive, it's fun, it's ordained by G-d himself and well, it's the once a week par-tay.

After dinner, even before after-dinner grace or "benching", Jonathan retrieves his M-16 from the pile. He climbs the west tower every night to stay up guarding the village. He says he prays and screams to keep himself awake all night long. "Around three in the morning is the worst. That is when it is the coldest, and I get real sleepy, so I just scream auuughhhh into the wind," he says. He grabs pastries with one hand, slings the rifle over the opposite shoulder and leaves.

People stay for benching, then the dinner winds down. Some Yeshiva students light cigarettes off the candles and wander off to their various houses.

In the morning, Yocheved shows up at Carol's house and takes me with her to her Shul. Somehow I learn to say Yocheved. "Yocheved must be someone important in the Bible who is she?" I ask.

"She was Moses' mother," Yocheved says.

"Wow! I had no idea."

The morning service parsha 'BeShalach' is read in Hebrew exactly like in America. The only thing different is the prayer books to follow along do not have translations, let alone transliterations; so I have no idea what they are reading.

My new best friend, Yocheved and I head back to the kitchen for the second meal of Shabbat. She's a Texas girl, who moved to Israel in her early thirties. She got married and the blonde beauty is her daughter, Chaiki. At least the other girl's name is easy to say, Sarah, her adopted daughter. Yocheved was also a cheerleader in America growing up. Like me, she had cheered for the Friday night games. Later in life we had both found Orthodoxy to be the way to go. She is much stricter than I, but we understand each other and get along famously. She tells me when I am doing something wrong, and usually why. Plus she reads, writes, and speaks Hebrew.

Back in the kitchen, we help set up the second meal. Mike does the bread and wine blessings. He then goes into the actual kitchen, we call the dining room "the kitchen." Just like the Tapuach summit is not at the top of the hill, but rather the bottom, the dining room is known as the kitchen—just some weird Israeli anomalies of language.

Mike brings out his famous barley-laden "cholent" stew and he serves it, or we do, or somehow it is served in bowls for everyone.

"This is Lenny. He is studying at Yeshiva and has a lecture on the story of Devorah,"

Mike says. He sits, and Lenny stands to shed light on the week's lesson.

"Is this the parsha reading this week?" I ask Yocheved.

"Yeah," she says.

"I did not do this on purpose. I was supposed to arrive here last week, but British Airways forgot to heat the cargo hold so I had to delay until this week," I say.

"That is too weird."

"It's like karma or something. Seriously, you can't make this up," I say.

Yocheved smiles and we both listen to Lenny's studied interpretation.

Sunday comes, and as per Mike's Saturday decree, he is going into town. I am in the kitchen early finishing my coffee when he announces that fifteen minutes he is leaving for Ariel.

The rusty, red-dirt encrusted blue van quickly fills to capacity with riders. Near the gate of K'far Tapuach is a bus stop where we pick up a hitchhiker; then at the bottom of the hill, at the summit Tapuach, we pick up yet another hitchhiker. We are squashed in the van together. It seems when you are sharing and helping others by giving rides, that the entire vehicle is under divine protection from G-d, due to your kindness. Therefore, everyone always wants to help a hitchhiker.

In Ariel, some people get off and continue on by bus, or hitchhike to Jerusalem or Tel

Aviv or wherever. We go to a strip mall and find a hardware store. I buy a dozen three-inch long nails, but decide against buying a hammer because it is only a one-time use item. Instead, I go next door and buy a Hebrew–English dictionary with transliterations, a far better use of my "hammer money," I think to myself.

Then Mike, myself, and Jonathan have shwarma at what has to be Israel's best shwarma shop, probably even the best shwarma in the world. We watch as the man behind the counter slices long thin pieces of meat off the vertical spit. I think the meat is lamb, but it could be turkey, with all the spices it is hard to tell. You can get French fries stuffed into your shwarma for no additional charge, but if you want a side of fries, then you have to pay extra. I opt for the grilled eggplant instead. The little cubby hole restaurant is packed with villagers and soldiers who grab a quick meal on their way to their various destinations further into the West Bank.

On the way out of Ariel, we go past the guard shack and pull into the gas station at the base of a rather nice hotel. Between Mike, Jonathan, Moshe, Donnie and Tennessee, I am told the now deceased owner of the hotel got blown up by a suicide bomber at the gas station, only two months ago.

"He saved many people's lives because he was wrestling with the Palestinian terrorist, but the guy was able to set off his bomb," Moshe says.

"They have only just finished rebuilding the gas station," Jonathan says.

Everything looks perfect, new, nice, and shiny—as if nothing bad had ever happened.

There is no self-service at the gas station, an armed attendant pumps your gas, for security's sake. I am not noticing people with guns anymore, as they are so commonplace.

I ask Mike when I can get a gun. He says something about having to qualify at the range. I say, "Bring it," remembering Big Tony's lessons.

We get back to K'far Tapuach after letting off a couple of hitchhikers at the summit. Mike tells me that Moshe will be showing me around.

"I'll be right back, I need to take care of something at home," I say.

I leave the kitchen and head back to Carol's house. I take the dog out to pee, being careful to clip him onto a leash. Then, I take the nails, and try to use my shoe to nail the back door shut. It doesn't work. I look around and find a rock that won't crumble. I proceed to nail the door shut. There is also a window, so I nail the window in such a way that it can only open four inches. I try not to damage the trim around the door. I put nails at the top and the bottom of the door securing it permanently. Somehow, I don't think Carol will like that I nail her door and window, but as long as I have to live here, the door is shut. I return Po-poki to my bedroom so he can resume his hard work of sleeping on my bed.

I have begun to notice odd things about Carol. She has no refrigerator and often takes the big bowls of left-overs from the community kitchen and hides them under her sink. As the days go by, she tells me she is from different places: Los Angeles, New Orleans, Florida, and that she was a teacher, a secretary, or a soldier. She keeps giving both male and female clothing to Tennessee. We begin to tease him how she wants a boyfriend, and "you're it." Even one of my beanies goes missing, but I cannot prove anything. And why does she keep a pick axe and a shovel in the bathtub? She tells me that David Ha'iveri asked her to clean them up, but in the bathtub? Also, I constantly remind her I do not speak Hebrew.

Other times Carol tells me that David Ha'iveri had told her she is not allowed to speak, and she must just do whatever she is told. David seems to be a leader of sorts, as part of the Shomron Regional Council. I wonder if this village is some kind of weird cult, or if Carol is exaggerating. The next time I see David I look for any kind of sign that he is running around hypnotizing people like Jim Jones or something. Fortunately, I find nothing strange or unusual about David or even his wife Mollie;

who has told me numerous times that if I need anything to "just ask."

Right now, I do not have time to worry about Carol's eccentricities. I have to go meet Moshe and get the lay of the village. We walk the perimeter together with one of the dogs. He explains the different lookout points and their significance, the distance in kilometers to the Mosque we hear every night blasting Islamic prayers, and how the houses around the perimeter have bulletproof walls.

We work together a lot, doing guard duty or "shmira," and training the dogs in tracking. I use Po-poki to show how a track is laid and how dogs "get scent." Moshe has the maturity and patience to learn the slow process of K-9 mantracking.

Moshe picks one of the shepherds at the kennels and begins to work with him daily in tracking. He shares his IDF and Bedouin tracking skills, I share my hybrid American Indian/sheriff tracking skills. We talk a lot about our hopes for Israel, our families, our dreams, and wishes for the future.

I struggle with not wanting to tell Carol about nailing the window and door shut. I wasn't going to. Then I think, what if there is a fire and she tries to get out the back? Finally, I tell her about nailing her door shut, and window so it can't open all the way. She doesn't seem to care.

Chapter 6
Bed & Breakfast 2 Miles

Jan 12, 2003 - Eli Biton, 48, of Moshav Gadish is killed and four people wounded when terrorists infiltrate the community and open fire. Two terrorists are killed by Israeli forces. The Islamic Jihad claims responsibility for the attack.

Jan 12, 2003 - Corporal (Reserves) Mikhail Kazakov, 34, of Jerusalem is killed by terrorists who infiltrate across the Israel-Egypt border, near the Negev town of Nitzana.
www.jewishvirtuallibrary.org

The perimeter fence around the village is mostly chain link, with occasional spots of barbed wire. Everywhere holes in the fence present gaping spots where a previous infiltration had taken place. The despicable morning discoveries, hopefully without anyone having been murdered, are sometimes pieced back together with wire or garbage bag ties. At other times, nobody has any extra wire and they are left open, blank, vulnerable, staring back, as you walk past sections of holey fencing.

One side of the village has a military installation just outside and slightly downhill from the fence. Inside the village fence, on the side where there is lovely vegetable gardens, is Sephardic Jews. Lots of American ex-pat Jews live throughout K'far Tapuach.

Where the houses are, there are sidewalks. The rest is red dirt that clings to boots and pants. If you continue up the road leading to Tapuach a couple more kilometers, you run into the Arab village.

Ofttimes, we observe Red Crescent Ambulances unloading people who get magically healed once they hit their village. They jump up from lying prone on a gurney, pick up large boxes, and using great strength, carry them up the hill. Two men will huff and puff to unload rifle-sized boxes. Then, the "healed" man will stick the heavy wooden box on his head or back, and walk up the hill to their village. Other times half a dozen men and women will jump out of one of these Ambulances, everyone carrying bags with vegetables hanging out the top. I suppose it's nice that these Red Crescent Ambulances help everyone in the Muslim village get through roadblocks and go shopping.

Both Jews and Arabs share the road leading down to the summit Tapuach, where both catch their respective different busses from separate bus stops. Only the Jewish bus stops have shelters.

When elderly Arab women carrying large loads of groceries go and sit in the Jew's bus shelter, and a Jew kicks them out; of course Jews look bad. This makes all Jews look mean and petty for not letting grandma sit down or get out of the noonday sun. That is exactly why Arabs refuse to build shelters or benches for their bus stops. It is easy international brownie points, until you learn the sneaky truth.

There are yellow license plate busses for Jews and green plates for Arabs. If an Arab gets on a Jewish bus, he or she will be harassed and taunted. If a Jew gets on an Arab bus, they will get murdered, or worse.

It is about a mile hike from the village of Tapuach down to the summit Tapuach. It is not safe for Jews to walk the road because one can get ambushed and, then again, murdered. Muslims walk it all the time.

One early morning, after we had been out tracking all night, we slide the side door of the van open, and let the two K-9s bark incessantly. We sarcastically offer a ride to a terrified

Muslim woman. Tennessee, who had been asleep, wakes at the sound of the dogs.

"You don't shit where you eat," he says, and demands us to stop.

"Waddah ya mean?"

"We live here, and we don't need any extra trouble around the village," he says. Our gleeful revenge is cut short.

Muslim vehicles drive around with electrical tape on the windshields saying "TV" in big black letters. Guess we aren't supposed to question their fake TV reporter vehicle. Sometimes the electrical tape says UN. Other times, a real UN vehicle—with some stupid rape-bait western liberal—will go to borders to harass and scream at the IDF as searches are conducted on Muslims. Why are the Jews searching Muslims and not fellow Jews? Oh, could it be because the Muslims like to blow up Jews and other Infidels? Their favorite explosive is called "Mother of Satan" because it is so volatile that accidently jiggling it makes it blow up. Inept bomb makers are all the time blowing themselves up trying to learn this new skill set.

On my way to meet with Moshe, I pass two men working on an electrical transformer box. Both have black Glocks strapped to their waistbands. One is elbow deep in the box working on multi-colored wires; the other stands about five feet back. His M-16 held snug to his body, he constantly surveys the surrounding terrain. He stands ready to instantly defend his fellow electric company employee. "Shalom," we both nod at each other. The guy working in the box doesn't even notice my passing.

I meet Moshe and we exchange pleasantries. We begin to walk the perimeter of the village.

"Why do they leave these things around?" I ask Moshe about the giant metal and concrete boxes around the perimeter. I assume they are left over pieces of heavy machinery that goes to an earthmover or tractor. A lot of them have hinges like they hook onto maybe a crane or something. You'd think they would pick them up and take them to the next job, and not just leave them lying around, I think.

"Those are like a... How do you say, a place where the army hides and shoots?" Moshe says.

"Like a foxhole. No, a bunker. A bunker, that's it. I think it's called a bunker," I say. I look again at the next oval box we come to with new eyes. I can see where you can hide in what I had only moments before thought to be leftover equipment. I think of a Clint Eastwood Cowboy movie where one naive guy is talking to Clint. He thinks the residents of the house must be religious because they have crosses on all the windows. Clint Eastwood corrects the dummy. He explains how the crosses aren't religious, but gun ports which allow the person inside to shoot in all directions.

There is a radio tower which is for the Arab village up the hill. Me, I would cut the darn thing down, but I think they leave it up so they can listen in on the Muslims. You know, learn if they are planning a bombing or something. All around the radio tower is barbed wire in rolls, layer upon layer, round circular spirals. It's not double layered, but about ten layers deep, at least eight feet wide and four feet high.

Up one of the highest hills of the village is called the migdol mayim or water tower. It is not a tower but a tank. Just like the summit is at the bottom and not the top of the hill, the tank is called a tower.

This is the water source for the village. I don't know how much it pumps per minute, but the barbed wire is about twenty feet thick and over eight feet high, with a double chain link fence in addition. Like Mark Twain said, "Whiskey's for drinkin' and water's for fightin'." I look at the water tower and it's evident someone is very willing to fight for this.

"Why do you wear those pants?" Moshe asks me.

I think, not again. I have to explain to yet another villager why I am wearing pants and not a long skirt. I had brought long sleeve shirts, specifically to not offend seriously Orthodox people, and was always careful to cover my head at all times. Granted, it was only a baseball cap, with a pony tail braid hanging out the hole, but it was something. I had already explained to Mike and a number of other people, "I am not going to sprint after a dog on rough terrain, tracking a terrorist, while wearing a skirt. I could trip and fall down. It is life threatening for me to wear a skirt." I start the same spiel for Moshe.

He cuts me off. "No, why do you wear that color of pants?"

"The color?"

"Yes, the black and white."

"Well, I have trained for Urban Search and Rescue. That is what I figured I would be doing, like earthquakes and bombings. If you are searching for days, like 9/11, you get dirty. You won't have time to change your clothes, or room to carry extra pants. You could probably carry an extra T-shirt in your pack and change that. Then you would feel fresh, and the black and white urban camo would hide the dirt on the bottom. So, you will feel clean, which will boost your morale in a terrible situation." I am actually quite surprised he asked. And, I am proud of my brilliant idea.

"That is the color of the Palestinian army," Moshe says.

"Oh my G-d!" I say. *Now I know why the woman with the baby said, "Don't shoot!"*

"Is something wrong?" Moshe asks.

I am too embarrassed to tell him about the woman, and my walking into the wrong house.

I say no and keep walking past some of the fence dogs. The noisy stray mutts are chained along one section of fence in a primitive alarm system. They bark at us. I am glad for their noise so I do not have to talk. I never wear the black and white camo again. I do not throw them away, but rather pack them in the bottom of my suitcase. That way I can be confident that no Palestinian gets a free uniform—at least not from me.

We come to a sign. It says "Bed & Breakfast 2 Miles" with an arrow pointing out to the desert and bare rocky mountains. A tiny dot in the distance shows a village.

"Is there a Bed and Breakfast out there?" I have visions of some fabulous oasis, a secret resort with massages, palm trees, and tropical fruit. In my mind, I am already planning on sneaking off to this paradise.

"Ah, no," Moshe says.

"Why does it say Bed & Breakfast?"

"Somebody put the sign, to make a funny," Moshe says.

"What is the village, way off there?" I ask.

"It's an Arab village."

"Oh."

Back at the kitchen, I make a cup of instant coffee. Moshe and Mike discuss something in Hebrew. Then Mike shows me the kitchen part of the kitchen and asks me if I know about kosher, the red and blue. I tell him yes. He then tells me that I am to be the cook.

"What? Oh, I knew you guys were going to try and put the chick in the kitchen. How did you handle the cooking before I showed up?"

"Oh, everyone took a week and we rotated," Mike says.

"Well, I did not come here to cook! You can hire anyone to do that! I came here to train dogs for tracking and protection! I have worked at this for over five years steady. I've had training all over California, New Mexico, Nevada, and Colorado. I took Emergency First Responder courses for nine months. I took earthquake simulator classes, rubble pile classes, bomb classes, wilderness classes, and sheriff academy classes in man-tracking. I worked with police, sheriff, highway patrol, border patrol, rangers, FEMA, DOT, FBI, OES. I can show you my training books. I got three binders full of my trainings. I didn't take one cooking class. I took all these dog classes and you want me to cook? I have taken so many dog classes I don't even remember everyone I trained with, but you want me to cook? I did not come here to cook, but to train dogs, and that is exactly what I am going to do! I will take my week rotation just like everyone else, but I will not be responsible for the cooking other than my rotation!" Then I leave.

Outside away from the kitchen, I telephone my husband and repeat the loud monologue I just gave Mike. When I finish, John tells me that our Chabad Shul back in Marina Del Rey is chained shut. He doesn't really know what happened, only that they aren't there. He says everyone is acting weird, but not talking about it, so he isn't sure why it is shut. He tells me he is going to go over to the Rabbi's house next Friday night. I remind him to tithe "because I need all the blessings and protection I can get."

Maybe it is PMS or bad karma, but back at Carol's house, I open the door to find Po-poki running around the house, again. I had carefully left him in my bedroom and here he is happily sniffing around the living room and kitchen. Carol comes in the door. I ask her if she had let the dog out of my bedroom.

"Oh, he's so cute. I was only playing with him, and just let him stay in the living room," she says in a high-pitched girly voice. She twirls a loose strand of hair with her fingers, and then stuffs it under her head scarf.

She doesn't seem to understand that he is not a pet, but a working dog. He is not to be played with. He needs to stay in his crate, unless he's working. Carol continues talking in an abnormal child's voice. I do not know why some women do that, but if there is one thing I cannot stand is a grown woman talking in a sickening-sweet child's voice. A breathy baby-talk voice is more appropriate for a skinny blonde bimbo in a mini skirt, but here I am looking at the antithesis, cringing at every word.

"Well, what if I go by his crate and he is whining to go out, can I just open the front door and let him go outside?"

"NO! He is a working dog! He must be on leash at all times! He will run away because he gets a scent of something and just goes. He only whines because he sees you," I say. I repeat the same things over and over. Nothing is penetrating. Carol keeps talking in that little girl voice.

"But if he's whining he needs to go outside and pee. I could open the door and just let him out real quick to pee," she pleads.

"NO! He only whines because he sees you. Do not go in my room and he won't whine. He doesn't need to go out. I take him out three or four times a day. He's fine. Do not mess with him," I say. She keeps droning on and on about wanting to let him out. I catch myself repeating myself, to no avail.

I clip the dog onto a leash. "I have to go to the kennels." I leave.

I release a deep breath of frustration, walk over to the kitchen, and ask some Yeshiva boys where Yoni is, the main dog trainer. They tell me he is over at the kennels, exactly where I thought he was. So I go there.

When I find Yoni, I practically attack him trying to explain how he must talk with Carol regarding my dog. I am a bit panic-stricken about my dog running off due to some idiot's idea that he is a pet. Yoni, every bit the soldier and gentleman, calmly listens. I beg Yoni to talk some sense into her.

I explain about Carol, "She wants to let the dog go outside, but my dog cannot be off leash. He will run away, because he is a man-tracking dog. Could you please try to explain to Carol because I am not making any headway with her?" I make the hand signal for Po-poki to sit. Po-poki stops sniffing Yoni's pant leg and sits.

"If she hears it from a man, she will probably listen. She keeps talking in this little girl voice," I say. "When grown women talk baby talk it's because they have some kind of daddy problem. They listen to men more than women. She will listen to you because you're a man. You have to talk to her."

Yoni says he will "handle it and have a talk with her."

Right now, we clean up the kennels, rotating dogs into empty cages as we clean them. We then rinse and repeat, until all the cages are scrubbed down. While I do this, Po-poki has to be placed in one of the empty cages. He doesn't like it at all, and stands perfectly still—directly in the center of the cage. He refuses to lie down or even sit. He just stands there staring at me as if I have betrayed him.

After we finish with the cleaning we do some training with the K-9s. Then we both head back to the kitchen for dinner. I leave my dog still standing in the kennel until after dinner, when Yoni can talk with Carol.

At night, I dream Po-poki is running free in the wild scrub-brush hills of the West Bank. He ends up in an Arab village. A couple of young male villagers lure him close, then they whip out a huge jeweled knife and slice his ear off. Next, I am standing there with Po-poki's ear in my hand. I try to superglue it back on. I think, if that doesn't work, maybe I will cut off the other ear so at least the dog won't be lopsided.

Chapter 7
Showdown at Midnight

> Jan 17, 2003 - Netanel Ozeri, 34, is killed when terrorists enter his home, in an outpost north of Kiryat Arba, and open fire. His 5-year-old daughter and two friends are wounded. Hamas claims responsibility for the attack.
> *www.jewishvirtuallibrary.org*

Tonight, when I walk into the house, Carol shows me a puppy. A mutt of undefined breed, cute like all puppies, she cuddles it. The next thing she tells me is she is going to train it for man-tracking "just like your dog."

So, I ask her if she knows anything about dog training. She doesn't. Does she even know what breed the dog is that she holds? She doesn't.

Then she informs me "it is no problem." She plans to follow me around with her new dog and do exactly what I do.

"That's impossible," I say, firmly. "That is not how you train a tracking dog! My dog is fully trained, and that is a puppy! There is no way he can run behind us when my dog gets scent. It is not even physically possible. It would be completely dangerous. When my dog runs full speed I can barely keep up—holding the leash! And you expect a puppy to follow a full-grown dog? That dog doesn't even know how to sit. It's not even potty trained. Your dog would only be playing and you will be constantly picking him up when he gets tired."

I take a breath and look for signs she is understanding. "You don't even know if he has the drive to do this kind of work. Without knowing what the parents are, there is no way to tell if this dog even has the predisposition for this work. No, you will not be following behind me! And NO, I will NOT potty train your puppy!" Somewhere in this speech she gives a few "buts . . ." and "what if . . ." in her best little girl voice.

I go into my room to make some quick entries in my journal. I plug my Mac computer into the black 1940s converter that has to weigh twenty-five pounds or more. Pinner had given it to me last week. I look at the tall, heavy, brick-sized converter, and then at the burnt plastic 1/100th of an ounce modern converter and wonder what had happened to American know-how. The ancient converter, made in an era when American ingenuity was at its prime, still works. The modern Chinese imitation never worked.

I feed and take Po-poki out for potty break. Back in my room, I leave the computer plugged in. I carefully lock my bedroom door with the key Yoni had given me. I turn the modern skeleton key three times to the left. Then, realizing it is the wrong direction, I unwind it three times and turn it three more times in the opposite direction. I shake and try the door to make sure it is locked after I finish. I look at the cute puppy in the box set up in the living room. I head over to the kitchen for breakfast.

Yoni, the current trainer in a long line of dog trainers, left a couple of days ago. Rumor has it that he is headed to New Zealand, but who knows. He is just one of the latest dog trainers, volunteers, and Yeshiva boys coming and going.

A couple of Yeshiva boys are assigned to the kennels. They are on dog food duty. I hope they do their job and don't forget to feed the dogs like the last ones who had forgotten over Shabbat. I had scolded them last Saturday in the only language they knew, the Bible.

"It says in the Bible your animals have to be fed *before* you eat, not after, or when you feel like it. Besides, these are special dogs that are meant to protect Jews. The least you can do is feed them. If you can't do that, at least tell someone, so someone else can feed them."

"Where does it say that?" Yeshiva boy challenges.

"I dunno, somewhere. I didn't bring my Bible, so I can't show you."

"There is some over there," Mike chimes in, looking up from his newspaper. He points to the corner table laden with Siddurs and Tanakhs.

"Those are in Hebrew and I can't read Hebrew," I say. Yeshiva boy slams the door on his way out.

"Why do you refer to it as 'Bible'?" Mike asks.

"It's easier than saying Torah, Kethuvim and the Navi'im."

"Why didn't you bring your Bible then?"

"I left it home on purpose because it is the King James Bible, and I thought you would get upset if I had a King James Bible. I didn't want you to think I am a missionary trying to convert you, or something."

"Why don't you just get an Old Testament?" Mike says.

"I don't think they make them. I looked all over the Internet. You can get only a New Testament, but I couldn't find just the Old Testament in English. You can find it in Hebrew but not in English."

"There are inaccuracies in the King James."

"Well, it is the best I can do right now, since I don't read Hebrew."

Later in the week, he presents me with an Old Testament in Hebrew and English. Right now, the kitchen fills up with other volunteer dog handlers and trainers. Mike announces we are requested to escort the body of Netanel Ozeri who has just died, more specifically, has just been murdered. We are to all wear our T-shirts, the green "Gedud Ha'iveri" or Jewish Guard T-shirts and jackets he had given us. We are to meet in front of the kitchen in an hour.

Then Mike starts talking in Hebrew. I zone out. I look at Mike and the Yeshiva boys starting morning prayers in Hebrew. I wait for a break and say, "Amen."

I leave to change into the green T-shirt. I choose to wear black BDU's, since it is a funeral. I safety pin a Red Cross patch onto my mini back pack that holds first aid equipment, binoculars, and a small hand-held radio. I fill up two of my plastic water bottles in the sink outside the bathroom and shove them into the side slots of the pack. The whole pack fits neatly on my hips. Passport in a pouch around my neck inside the new T-shirt, I'm ready.

Outside the kitchen, people are milling around. Some are smoking. Others talk quietly. I sit on the stone retaining wall and wait for Mike to show up in the dirty blue van. When it arrives, it is filled dangerously overweight, with far too many people for comfort.

We take highways and side winder streets. The army has blocked off access to areas where people want to go to attend this funeral. Someone is reading a map. Someone else is talking and pointing, mostly Hebrew, so he must know the way. I look over his shoulder at the map in Hebrew and realize how completely illiterate I am.

We let about half a dozen people off on a corner, slightly away from the roadblock, out of view of the soldiers and police. Mike parks under some trees and we decide to walk to the funeral. Tennessee, Donnie, Moshe, Jonathan, myself, a couple Yeshiva boys, and Mike hop out of the van. We do a quick radio check and clip our radios onto our belts or jacket collars. Mike leads the way.

We walk for a long time at a steady clip. Next, we go through terraced vineyards. I get winded, but Mike burrows ahead. I strain to keep up. We walk past homes of Muslims. We are in a Muslim village in the middle of Muslim farms. Covered women stand outside their adobe huts and quickly duck inside the smooth doorways as we approach. Jonathan, Moshe, and the Yeshiva boys have left us and taken a different route. Donnie and Tennessee are convinced that Mrs. Muslim is going inside to get a gun to shoot us. We keep climbing up the stepped farmlands. Occasionally we see a male Muslim who also ducks quickly into his home. I hold onto Mike's jacket, Orthodox protocol be damned. He's the only one left in our small group who speaks Hebrew and no way am I going to get separated.

We reach a plateau. It doesn't look like much. There is a driveway and a small hut. Tiny two-inch diameter trees line the steep dirt driveway. Ozeri's home looks similar to the Muslim homes we passed, only smaller.

Smoking, quiet conversations in Hebrew, more smoking, standing around, then a decision is made. Mike tells me to follow him. A couple Yeshiva boys also tag along. The way back to the van via the road is much quicker. For whatever reason, maybe because the roads are blocked, but more and more cars with grieving people have arrived. There are lots of people walking toward his mud hut. He must know a lot of people, I think to myself.

We find the van and get in. We start to drive to the home where the father, husband, teacher was murdered. All of a sudden, Mike drives the blue van straight across a field! It is an empty field for sure, but the old van is no four-wheel drive vehicle. We get stuck in the mud. He spins the tires.

"Stop!" I yell.

"We need to get out of the mud," he screams back at me, gunning the engine harder.

"You are making it worse, just stop. This isn't going to work!" I fling the door open while he is still gunning the engine. I jump out. The Yeshiva boys also get out. We look at the tires. The front are okay but the back are in mud up to the rims.

"What you need to do, is put it in drive, then reverse, then drive, then reverse, but you gotta do it fast and even," I say. He guns the engine. He doesn't understand my explanations for how to rock a car out of the mud. Neither Yeshiva boy knows how to drive.

"Here, let me drive, I'll show you. It's not so easy with stick, but I'll show you."

Mike gets out of the driver's seat and I hop in. He questions if I know how to drive.

"I live in California. Of course I can drive." I check where to shift for reverse and first, then proceed to show him how to shift back and forth while keeping a steady foot on the gas. We switch again. The Yeshiva boys and I try to push every time Mike shifts into first gear. None of this works. We are now stuck up to the axles.

The Yeshiva boys light cigarettes and look at the back end of the van. It is getting dark. I look around on the ground and in the immediate area for any kind of sticks. I find some old dry grass and a few sticks that I shove under the rear tires.

"What on earth are you doing?" Mike asks in a tone that shows he clearly thinks I am insane.

I try to tell him we have to find something for the tires to grab onto, to get some traction. "Even rocks might help." The Yeshiva boys continue smoking cigarettes, lighting new ones on the old. We are in mud up to our knees. Our efforts are in vain and one tire seems to be sunk down even deeper. Mike leaves on foot.

In no time, Mike comes flying back in an army Jeep with four soldiers. Discussions in Hebrew, then they all try to manhandle the van out of the mud. The Yeshiva boys help, but it's no use. Then, more discussions in Hebrew. The soldiers split up in four directions and now they too look for sticks. The headlights and side-mounted flashlights of the green Jeep illuminate the area. The soldiers find lots of sticks and shove them under the tires, exactly like I was doing. *When I do it, it's crazy, but when the army does it, it's brilliant! Hmmph!* They tie a rope from the van's bumper to the back of the Jeep and one soldier drives while the rest of us push the van up and out of the mud hole.

The soldiers bid us adieu. We jump into the van and head up the hill to Ozeri's lonely house. I hadn't noticed the size of the crowd that gathers. It is huge. Everywhere Orthodox men and women are screaming, crying, tearing shirts, filling all the surrounding hills and wadis. I recognize the prayer for the dead coming from some people. Others are holding books of Psalms praying, sobbing, howling. The women in their long gathered skirts, mud on the bottom ruffles are weeping and hiding their faces in books of Tehillim. It looks like Woodstock, only with religious Orthodox youth.

We arrive at the widow's home. She is not crying, but seems rather stoic for a woman who had barely last night witnessed her husband shot dead.

Friday night and there was a knock at the door. Her husband opened the door to their tiny mud home, hoping to have the honor of sharing his Sabbath meal with a guest. Two Palestinians shot him dead, when he opened the door. His wife and five children stare at their father, her husband, crumpled in a bloody mess.

I wouldn't be as calm as she. I think I would still be screaming. She isn't.

Mike and some of the men are arguing with the army, arms gesture for emphasis in typical Middle Eastern fashion. Nobody knows what is going on. Nobody has time to translate. The widow says something, and then stomps into the house. The body is wrapped in prayer shawls, white cloth, blue stripes, fringes, hide the sage's face.

The army does not want Ozeri buried on the hill. The wife tries to fulfill her husband's wishes. He wants to be buried on the hill. More arguing, pleading, Psalms. Then, a decision. A board is found for the body which is then carefully loaded into the van. Mike drives, and the wife rides in the passenger seat. We follow on foot. Hundreds of cars follow in a slow motion, sad procession, down the hill. Someone tells me we are going to Jerusalem.

When we get to the highway, those of us on foot are loaded into various follow cars. Every exit from the freeway is blocked with IDF vehicles, so we cannot turn off anywhere.

Someone tells me how if a body is buried on a hill, that the hill is now Jewish, and the same goes for Palestinians. It seems confusing to me because it is all Israel, yet these Phakestians are demanding they own a part of it. I think maybe they are afraid of ghosts or something. That must be why they won't bother a hill if a Jew is buried there.

At least three times, the procession turns around and heads back to the hill where Netanel was murdered.[2] Each time, I am told the widow has changed her mind and demands

---

[2] Throughout this incident I thought we were traveling between Jerusalem and Netanel Ozeri's hilltop home when in reality, according to Wikipedia we were traveling between Hebron (just outside Jerusalem) and Ozeri's home. The Wikipedia description of the funeral is wholly inaccurate in that the grieving friends and family absolutely did not "expose the face of Netanel Ozeri." These are very Orthodox and pious people who would never go against Torah principles, except to save a life.

he be buried there on the hill of their home. I am confused by the ordeal, and I'm hungry. I dig in my pack and find some power bars. I split them up and pass them to the guys.

It is dark, and we have presently turned around for the third and final time. We are headed for what I think is Jerusalem. Again.

We come to a bridge. We stop. There is a roadblock on the bridge. We are facing Yasomniks. They are a division of police which is made up mostly of big Russian Jews who are known for using Billy clubs to crack skulls and quell any kind of protest. We get out of the car and head up toward the blue van with the body. It is the lead car. Directly opposite, a row of Yasomniks stand dressed in black. They slap their Billy clubs intimidatingly into opposite palms and stare at us menacingly.

Someone asks me something. He doesn't speak English, and I do not speak Hebrew. He then points to my water bottle and indicates he wants a drink. I hand him the bottle. He takes a sip and hands it back, only a tiny sip, just enough to keep him going. He thanks me in Hebrew, then side curls swing around as he turns to leave. He must have been extraordinarily thirsty to even ask me, let alone drink from a woman's water bottle, I think to myself.

I have no idea what is being said, but I do know when someone loves to hurt people. These Yasomniks clearly love their job. I have no weapon and even if I did, I am no match for the six-footers.

I am told the Rabbi of Jerusalem is refusing for Netanel Ozeri to be buried in Jerusalem. The army, however, wants him buried in Jerusalem, but they have no rights to overrule the Jerusalem Rabbi. The wife and the dead scholar wants him to be buried where he died. The Jerusalem Rabbi refuses for him to enter Jerusalem after sundown.[3] The Yasomniks want to bust some heads.

"Let's go back to the hill and everyone is happy, except the Yasomniks," I say to Jonathan.

The Yasomniks clearly do not care that I am a woman, nor do they care I might be Red Cross. They will pound my skull in just for the fun of it. I search for an escape. If I jump off the bridge it is a long drop to the bottom. Most likely, I will break my neck. So that's out. I look around and it appears we are trapped in this narrow ravine.

There is always a way, I think to myself. Think, come on think.

I remember my self-protection class in college. My female teacher, a Judo black belt, used

---

[3] According to Jewish law, a body must be buried before sundown (or before sunup in some rulings.) Bringing a dead body into Jerusalem presents its own halacha problems.

to tell us girls, "There is always a way out of a situation. Use your head. Take off your shoes and throw them at the bad guy, or throw your books at the bad guy. Then, you can run away."

I look at all the vehicles around me. The cars are too low to the ground for me to roll under, so I check out the trucks. The big army trucks have enough clearance for me to easily slide under and avoid any Billy clubs. I decide if any fighting breaks out, I will duck and roll under the closest truck, and be careful to avoid the tires so it doesn't run me over.

Finally, the Chief Rabbi of Jerusalem concedes and allows Netanel Ozeri to be buried in Jerusalem. A slight scuffle breaks out, but the Yasomniks back down and let us pass. We get to the graveyard where Psalms are said. The Warrior Mystic is finally buried.

Exhausted, those from Tapuach pile back into the former hearse—our beloved decrepit dirty blue van. Everyone is spent, hungry, and thirsty. I pass the rest of my water around.

We drive on into the night. Miraculously, we find a store on this lonely drive. The neon lights flash and glow in the front of the store. Mike buys half a dozen large soda bottles, which we greedily pour into plastic cups. Someone says a quick blessing and we slurp down. Not much is available but chips and Bamba so we hungrily eat the empty calories.

Mike turns to us Americans and says, "This is why you came to Israel."

"This is NOT why I came to Israel; I did not come to attend funerals!" I say. I came to prevent funerals!"

Everyone gets quiet. Then, Jonathan says he got hit in the back of the head by one of the Yasomniks. I put on blue rubber gloves and check his bloody matted head for broken bones. I use my small flashlight to check his pupils for signs of concussion and tell him to let me know if he feels funny or sleepy. I offer to clean it up back at Tapuach, as there's not much I can do in the van.

He says he called the short Ethiopian Yasomnik "a monkey."

"Why would you say that?" I ask.

"Because he just follows orders like a little monkey."

"He probably has short-man complex."

"So," Jonathan says.

"He was probably trying to prove himself to the big guys on his team. All you did was give him exactly the motivation to test his baton."

"I don't care, he's still a monkey," Jonathan snaps.

The ride home is silent after the late night snacks. People doze or sit quiet, lost in their own thoughts, their own mortality, their own exhaustion. The black sky blends into the black landscape. The engine hums.

We get home after 4:00 A.M. I try to sneak in without waking Carol. I really do not want to chit chat. I want bed, and I want it two hours ago. Po-poki is waiting patiently, so I take him out. Then I feed and water him and take him out again. I fall worn out into bed.

Around six in the morning, I hear pots banging in the kitchen. It doesn't stop, so I go out of my bedroom to see what Carol is doing or what is going on.

"I dropped a pot," Carol says.

"Okay" Then I ask her where the puppy is. She doesn't want to talk about it. "What happened to the puppy?" She tells me how she was trying to keep it quiet, so it wouldn't bother me while I slept. This gets me more concerned. *Did she smother it?*

I ask her numerous times, but every time she says simply, "I don't want to talk about it."

I try in different ways to ask the same question trying to get her to tell me what she did with the dog. The box is gone and so is the puppy. My sleep deprived imagination tries to figure out what happened to the dog. "I gotta go back to sleep. I'm exhausted."

I go back into my bedroom. *She dropped a pot. I just need some sleep. I'll deal with the puppy later.*

About half hour later, just as I'm hitting REM sleep, I hear what sounds like someone in our kitchen violently throwing pots and pans onto the floor. I lie in bed hoping it's a dream. Then, I begin to hope she stops "dropping pots."

It becomes clear she is not stopping. She is slamming pots and pans onto the floor. I won't be getting any sleep.

"Aw, hell no! That's it." I get up. I violently swing the bedroom door open. "Look, I don't know what your problem is, but if you have a problem with me, you can just tell me! We can discuss this like normal people. You don't have to throw pots and pans onto the floor like a crazy woman!" She continues to throw pots on the floor like she is in a trance. She bends over again, picks up a pot, and re-throws it onto the floor.

"Oh, eff this shit, I'm outta here." I quickly go back into my room and put on pants, shirt and jacket over my long Johns. I snatch my backpack, stick my computer, phone, passport, money, and address book into it. I grab gloves, stick a beanie on my head, clip the dog onto a leash, and slam the door.

The wind takes my breath away. I shake and twist my hands into leather gloves, holding the leash under my arm. White swirls follow me and Po-poki as we walk away from the noise.

I figure Mike will try to talk me into making up and going back to live with Ms. Psychotic. "I'll just move into the dog kennels," I think. The biting cold freezes my face. As I approach the community kitchen, I think, "But for right now, I'll just go and sleep on one of the couches in the kitchen. I'll tell Mike about my move to the kennels in the morning."

Chapter 8
When You Sleep With Dogs

Jan 23, 2003 - Corporal Ronald Berer, 20, of Rehovot; Corporal Assaf Bitan, 19, of Afula; and Staff-Sergeant Ya'akov Naim, 20, of K'far Monash are killed by terrorists while on patrol south of Hebron. Hamas claims responsibility for the attack.

www.jewishvirtuallibrary.org

"What are you doing here?" asks Mike, waking me up.

"That woman is insane."

"Oh, maybe you could—"

I cut him off. "Of course I can't get along with her. Nobody can." I don't give him time to say anything more than one word. "She's a danger to me and my dog, and I will not live with her. That's the definition of crazy, when you are a danger to yourself or others, and she's crazy! Besides, I think she killed her dog."

"What dog?"

"She had some puppy and she said she was going to follow me around and train it for mantracking. This morning the puppy was gone. She said she was trying to keep it quiet so it wouldn't bother me. She refuses to tell me what happened to the dog. She keeps saying she doesn't want to talk about it. I think she killed it. Plus, she was throwing pots and pans on the floor!"

"What are you going to do?" asks Mike.

"I'm moving into the dog kennels."

"You can't live there, it's cold and there is no electricity," Mike says.

"This is supposed to be the scare tactic," I think to myself. "I already figured it out. I'll hang blankets all around one of the cages to help keep in the heat and for privacy. Maybe I can run an extension cord from the outside lights. It'll be like camping." I look at Mike and he isn't surprised by this at all. "Wait a minute, you knew this would happen! You knew she was unstable. You knew she was crazy, and you put me with her! This happened to all the other girls who roomed with her!"

Instantly the first conversation with Carol comes back. She had told me she was "soooo happy" to room with me because the other girls "were mean" to her. "They threw used tampons" at her. At the time, I had thought it is some kind of personal fight she had gotten into, maybe she was exaggerating. Perhaps a trash can had gotten spilled during an argument and she had taken it personally. I ignored the conversation at the time, thinking it was an overblown squabble.

"I thought you could get along with—"

I again cut him off. "I can't get along with her, nobody can. She's insane! And, I am moving into the dog kennels!"

"You can't move into the dog kennels!"

"Then you have to get me another place, or I'm sleeping in the kennels, tonight! Besides, she's not even a Jew!" *There, I blurted it out.*

Mike scolds me that I am "not qualified to determine who is or isn't a Jew."

How did I know she wasn't Jewish? Why did I think that? In a millisecond, my mind flashes to the only Reconstruction synagogue I had gone to. The African American cantor, who was leading the Friday night service because the regular Rabbi was sick, had tried to sham-wow us using Hebrew words and talk-story about his trip to Israel. The more he talked about Israel, the more we thought we are being conned. We wondered if it was even a synagogue at all.

His sales pitch only permanently closed the door to all Reconstruction synagogues, at least for me. During the snacks after service, he told us he was a recent convert. At the time, I wondered, if the conversion was authenticate, why did he have to prove how "Jewish" he was by talking about Israel? I thought, "if he did not go to Israel would he still be Jewish if the conversion was valid?"

That is exactly what Carol had been doing with all the Hebrew talk, when I clearly didn't understand a word, and kept telling her so. She dressed Orthodox and wrapped her hair in a married woman's manner even though she is not married. She did everything to convince others, or maybe herself, that she was Jewish.

"She's a convert. You're supposed to be nice to converts!" Mike says.

"Ah ha, I knew it! And, I was nice to her, but she's insane!

"Chas v' Shalom."

"You cannot convert a crazy person! She's crazy! She didn't only now get nutzo-bonko; this is something that has been happening for a long time. You know it is against the rules to convert crazy people. Therefore, she is not a Jew! It would be different if she got converted then something happened and she went crazy. Maybe she saw a bombing or something; but she is loony-bins and she's been this way for . . . well, who knows how long. This didn't just happen."

"Chas v' Shalom."

"Why does she insist on speaking Hebrew to me? To prove how Jewish she is?! More importantly, she is unbalanced and dangerous! She's a danger to me, and my dog."

I never spend any nights in the kennels. Mike puts me in Yoni's old house and has his roommate move in with another dog handler, temporarily. He has to figure out something fast with housing so limited. It would be improper to have the female dog handler room with any males so this did present a problem.

* * *

We are in the middle of the second intifada, and there is much news and talk about a war with Lebanon. It is funny how different countries report news. When I listen to American news if I can get it, I hear nothing unusual. When I listen to the BBC I get freaked out thinking Lebanon tanks are right outside my door. Russia must have made the war with Lebanon imminent.

My husband back in California hasn't heard a thing. Emmanuel's mother in Russia, hears all of this war talk, and insists he fly home. She worries about him. He stops going to classes at Ariel University so he can fulfill his mother's wishes. He gets free room and board for doing guard duty with the dogs. Overnight, he drops everything to fly home, leaving his Israel house empty. That is where I eventually end up.

I have barely finished cleaning Yoni's house, at least enough for me to live in. Now, here I am facing another bachelor pad. Emmanuel doesn't have a refrigerator and he leaves partially eaten jars and cans around. I have to throw out the half eaten cans of food so Po-poki doesn't get into them. They are all over the kitchen—on the counters, the floor, the tables, and the chairs.

Emmanuel's house is by far the dirtier of the two. I wonder if all Russians are so dirty. I quickly dismiss the thought as merely just another unmarried man's mess. I have no intention of cooking here, but I do clean up his kitchen, and organize all the salvageable jars of food. Pickles and olives I keep for him in a corner of the kitchen counter. "They should be okay, they're in vinegar," I think to myself. The herring in a cream sauce I am not sure about, so I wipe off the jar and put it with the rest of the jars, along with the pickled herring. I clean the table, wash his dishes and mop the floor. "If they keep moving me around, I will have cleaned every house in the village," I think as I clean.

The rest of the house has clothing strewn about. Dirty clothes are hard to distinguish from clean, so I re-wash them all, and fold them neatly on two chairs in the corner since he does not have a dresser.

The bathroom is a pig sty, so I scrub down the tub and toilet. Next to the toilet are the cardboard inserts of hundreds of rolls of toilet paper. I do not know what to make of it. Is he saving the cardboard for an art project? Why are they piled up to the top of the toilet tank? Is it insulation from the cold? As much as I brainstorm, I cannot figure a reason to save cardboard tubes from toilet paper. It looks like quite a collection. If he is saving them for a reason, then he surely will be upset if I throw them out. I glance at the now clean toilet with the cardboard tubes piled up behind the tank. "Hmmmm." I decide not to throw them out just yet.

The next day, I get Donnie, Tennessee, and Canada to help me get my stuff out of Carol's house. I refuse to return alone. They carry and wheel my dog crates and luggage down the street and around the corner to Emmanuel's house, as he is going to be gone for a couple of months.

I show them the collection of toilet paper tubes and ask them if there is any reason to save them. Nobody can come up with a good reason except Tennessee.

He says "Emmanuel probably took a picture of all the toilet paper rolls. He shows the picture to all his friends back in Russia, and brags 'look how rich I am in Israel. See, I have all this toilet paper I have used.'" We all giggle at our own cold war ideas of Russians. After a week or so, I finally throw them out.

Emmanuel later tells me he was "just too lazy to take them to the trash." He even laughs at Tennessee's joke, and says, "It's not like that anymore, in Russia."

* * *

Back in the kitchen, Mike asks for volunteers to stay at the widow's house and guard her. The arrangements are primitive. Mrs. Ozeri has two rooms in her hut, so our guys will be sleeping in a panel truck parked in the yard. About a half a dozen of our guys are going out to the hill to guard the widow from her unfriendly neighbors.

Mike wants to know why I am not volunteering. After all, "you are the one who is willing to sleep in the kennels."

I tell him "I think it would present sleeping problems, because I can't sleep with the guys in the truck and I don't think the widow has room for a guest in her home. So all the guys will have to sleep outside in the cold while I hog the truck?"

Big-Hair Josh makes himself a cup of coffee, carefully stirring in a couple of spoons of sugar. He takes a sip, then opens the front door and throws the coffee outside. He throws the cup away. I ask him why he keeps doing that.

"Because that woman keeps putting salt in the sugar bowl right next to the coffee." I look sideways at Mike and raise my right eyebrow. Mike pretends not to hear Josh, or notice my "told ya so" look.

My boots are pulling away from the seams. "They are only about a month old, but they are already splitting apart. They aren't supposed to split like that, they're Magnums," I say.

Someone tells me there is a shoe store in Ariel.

"I hope they have boots in my size. That would be a miracle in and of itself," I say.

Most of the guys set to guard at the widow's with K-9's, don't even have boots. None of their footwear is waterproof, mostly black dress shoes with leather soles. It is awfully muddy at the widow's house.

One of the Yeshiva boys complains, "My shoes aren't waterproof."

"I know how to make your shoes waterproof," I say.

I go into the kitchen and find all the pita bags I can. I pass them out to the dog handlers. "First you take off your shoes, now put these on over your socks, then put the shoe back on." The guys start to stick the bags over their socks. "Make sure you take them off when you sleep, so your feet can dry out from the sweat, and make sure to change your socks daily," I warn.

Mike wants to know where I learned this.

"When you grow up poor, you learn to make do with things," I say.

Mike drives the guard dogs, and handlers with bread-bag clad footwear out to the hilltop to protect the newly widowed woman and her children. There is no electricity on the hill. Nights settle in like rich black velvet, soft and silent. I am not sure about the bathroom facilities, but these young Jewish men mostly from New York City, are in for one a heck of a camping trip.

Chapter 9
To Be or Not to Be Jewish

Feb 6, 2003 - 2nd Lieutenant Amir Ben-Aryeh, 21, of Maccabim, and Staff-Sergeant Idan Suzin, 20, of Kiryat Tivon are killed and two more soldiers are wounded in a shooting attack in the area of Nablus. Both gunmen are killed by return fire from IDF troops. The Popular Front for the Liberation of Palestine and Fatah-Tanzim claim responsibility for the attack.

Feb 11, 2003 - Major Shahar Shmul, 24, of Jerusalem is killed by a Palestinian sniper near the Church of the Nativity in Bethlehem while checking a suspicious vehicle. The PFLP and the Islamic Jihad claim responsibility for the attack.

www.jewishvirtuallibrary.org

Some time ago, I took over the feeding of the dogs. Two times a day I take each dog out for a walk and basic training. Afterwards, I feed and water every dog. I cut through the village in such way so I can cover the entire perimeter twice a day. I use each dog to walk along a specific section of the fence. I now know every IDF guard at the front gate. They see me all the time walking with many different dogs. I avoid the section of fence where the chained fence dogs are, so as to avoid a dogfight.

Most of the shmira, or guard duty, is repetitive and boring—just walking a perimeter. Sometimes I am with another guard, but often I'm alone with a dog and my thoughts. I review basic commands with each K-9 twice a day. Like the feedings cannot take a break for Shabbat, neither can the trainings.

One particular night, Moshe is guarding with me. I have the dog and he has the M-16. We round the corner where the creepy nightly Muslim prayers can be heard echoing through the mountains.

On nights when there has been a shooting or other attack on Jews, the prayers seem extra excited, animated, and obvious to the point that even a non-Arabic speaker can tell they are saying something like "Hooray, we killed some Jews," or "Congratulations on killing Jews." I wonder to myself why the Israeli government allows these people to live here. They are vile killers, who's only loyalty is to the death and destruction of Israel. I truly don't understand why they would allow this, and nobody so far has been able to explain why.

"How far is Lebanon?" I ask, thinking about all the BBC news talk of imminent war.

"Two kilometers over that hill," Moshe says tipping his chin towards a mountain sitting left of the boisterous Mosque.

Our numbers have been cut in half since so many of the K-9 handlers left to guard the widow. We gain a few extra dog handlers or wanna be dog handlers from the latest batch of Yeshiva students visiting for Shabbat.

Two of the latest are Ari and Elchonon who just happens to be almost fully deaf. Tennessee begins his latest comedy skit which involves a blind guard and a deaf guard.

"Can you see anything?" Tennessee closes his eyes to show he is the blind guard.

"WHAT?"

"I said, can you see anything?" Tennessee says with eyes closed.

"HUH? I CAN'T HEAR YOU." Tennessee's deaf guard screams.

Again closing his eyes he would eventually scream "CAN . . . YOU . . . SEE . . . ANYTHING?"

He doesn't stop until everyone is laughing hysterically about the conversations between the imaginary deaf and blind guards. Guess that's what happens when you don't have TV.

* * *

At the Internet café in Ariel University, I look up the Magnum boot company. Since I do not have a printer, I handwrite a note to the Magnum company as neat as I can. I explain how I am training dogs in the West Bank for man-tracking etc. I do not recall the entire letter, just the closing line: "It is no fun tracking terrorists with wet feet." I find a box and put the boots with the now flapping soles in it with the note. I mail it back to the United States.

Mike is certain I just wasted postage, and can't figure out what they will possible do. I tell him they are going to send me some new boots. He doesn't believe it.

Meanwhile, I wear the boots I found at the shoe store in Ariel. They are not nearly as good, but they do seem to be waterproof. At least I have boots. The guys out guarding the widow only have bread bags over their socks. Their shoes still get soaked. The bread bags only keep the moisture off their feet. I look at the cheap boots I am wearing and even with the squishy soles, I give a little prayer of thanks.

While waiting for the bus back to Tapuach from Ariel, a little girl comes up to Canada and me. She wants to give us bumper stickers for some politician.

I ask if it is Ariel Sharon, the only politician I've ever heard of. I tell her "I like Ariel Sharon."

She says, "No, this guy is better." She still wants to give us bumper stickers.

We both refuse.

She insists we take the bumper stickers. Even when we say we do not have a car, she still demands, "Take it, just take it!" We have to take the bumper stickers from the bossy little girl.

"Man, you can sure tell a Jewish woman, even at eight years old!" Canada says.

* * *

Next day in Tapuach, I cut through the village during my morning training. Coming from one of the houses I hear Spanish. I stop to listen, because I can understand most of the conversation between the husband and wife. I think for a moment my ears are playing tricks on me and it's really Hebrew.

It is a weird thing, but whenever someone cannot speak English I immediately switch to first Spanish, then Hawaiian, and then run through the few phrases I know in French, or German. Here I am hearing Spanish. I am certain my ears are playing tricks. Who would be speaking Spanish in Israel?

"Como se llama?" I say to the man as he exits his house. He tells me his name which I promptly forget in my excitement. I can hardly believe I can communicate with someone in a language other than English. The Belgium shepherd sits politely while I converse with the man. He speaks Hebrew second language and Spanish first. I speak English first and Spanish second language.

Even though I forget Spanish words here and there, I find out he is Peruvian. Seems some village in Peru thought they were Jewish from the time of Isabel and Fernando who exiled the Jews from Spain in the 1400s. They sent word to Israel, who sent over some Rabbis to confirm their Jewishness. The Rabbis sent over were Orthodox. They ruled that the Peruvians were most likely halachaly Jewish. They also felt that too much time had passed since the people had practiced Judaism properly. So, they said the Peruvians should convert just to be on the safe side.

What happened next is amazing. This entire town in Peru converted to Judaism, then everyone packed up and moved to Israel. Talk about the ingathering. I leave off talking with the Peruvian man with a big grin on my face.

I pass the kindergarten where an IDF soldier is on guard. He is lying in the field slightly uphill from the front entrance. His weapon beside him aimed in the general direction of the playground. Wildflowers are beginning to bloom all around and he has an eight inch piece of wild wheat in between his teeth. He looks like a hillbilly relaxing on a haystack, waiting for Daisy Mae to show up. The M-16 is incongruous with his casual appearance.

I take the dog back to the kennels and feed all dogs. Then, I go by my house and get Popoki. I take him out for his morning walk/training, then I feed him also. Back at my house or Emmanuel's house, I decide I should mop the living room floor as it has gotten quite dirty from muddy boots and dog hair.

Israeli style of mopping is strange to American sensibilities, but it does get the job done. First, you pour about a cup or two of sudsy water on the tile floors, then using what looks like a giant squeegee on a mop handle, you scrape the water around picking up dirt into a black muddy pile. Yes, it is a little odd but it takes care of the sweeping and the mopping with one pass. After the squeegee water part, you take a dry towel or rag and wrap it around the squeegee and dry the floor.

That is how I find Emmanuel's Uzi. Yes I know. I am supposed to turn it in, but nobody asked and gosh darn it, the BBC keeps wigging me out with talk of imminent war with Lebanon. If caught with an unauthorized weapon, it means seven years in prison, do not pass go, do not collect two hundred dollars. And no, you do not get a court trial, just automatic prison, seven years. I look at the black stubby gun and think, "I would rather spend seven years in an Israeli prison than one second in a Muslim prison."

I hide the gun under the blankets on the bed which is where Po-poki sleeps all day long. At night, I keep it beside me in bed. Again, nobody asks, and I do not volunteer or show off. This helps me sleep much better at night.

Mike dilly-dallies for weeks about me getting a gun. Finally, he takes a bunch of us to the range. We are given a lecture on proper handling and usage. It is against the law to carry any gun with a bullet in the chamber. Big Tony had tried to explain this to me in California. I did not understand it then, but now it is clear.

The instructor tells us, "If you see a terrorist at 200 yards you must yell 'Achshav!' Then if they are still coming at 100 yards you must yell 'Achshav!' again. Then at 50 yards you yell 'Achshav!' and you can now shoot—but only into the ground in the direction of the bad guy. At 25 yards, you again yell 'Achshav!' and now you can shoot him in the leg. At 10 yards you may shoot at will but of course yelling 'Achshav!' the entire time.

Us Americans, sneak sideways looks at each other. Everyone, at least every American has incredulous, mouth agape, looks on their faces. At break, we all agree we will just shoot the terrorist, then yell 'Achshav!' the required four or five times.

"It's better to be judged by twelve, than carried by six," Tennessee says, summarizing all of our thoughts.

We shoot many different pistols. My cluster is the size of a fifty-cent piece, with only one upper right stray, thanks to Big Tony's lessons. In the Emergency First responder class back in LA, I knew I was going to Israel, and was complaining how I couldn't "hit the broad side of a barn with a shotgun."

Big Tony, a cop in Los Angeles, said he could "get me on paper." So for a month right before I left for Israel, I met with Big Tony and he trained me in tactical shooting. I bought the ammo and he trained me how to shoot and handle, guns. He taught me proper stances for shooting. He had some way of scoring the shots fired at the targets we used. Finally one day, he said I was "as good as LAPD sharpshooters." I was absolutely excited just to be able to hit the paper instead of the walls all over the gun range.

Even with good placement, Mike still comes up with some other excuse why I can't have a gun. I think it is something about having to "go to the army range and qualify with them."

I again say "Bring it," and keep my mouth shut about my secret find under Emmanuel's bed.

Mike is making a food run out to where our guys are guarding the widow. We pack all kinds of food for their Shabbat table. He has gotten extra challah and even sent them some wine and soup, ground beef, salads, paper products, and trash bags. He even throws in a couple of siddurs and song books

Mike and Daniel are discussing the heretical Kabbalah Centre with all the movie stars in LA.

I say, "I used to go there, and if it weren't for the Kabbalah Centre that I would not be Orthodox. Now I got to the Chabad but it was the Kabbalah Centre that got me started on the Orthodox route."

"Why did you stop going there?" Daniel asks.

"Because they started catering to wealth and influence, and even to non-Jews over Jews who might be poorer," I say. "Neither my husband nor I liked watching the leaders fall over themselves kissing up to celebrities."

"They say it's a cult," Mike says.

"Probably is, but there's a lot of Jews who returned to Judaism due to the influence of the Kabbalah Centre," I say.

There is much more to this conversation regarding oral law vs. written law. I bring up the child's game of telephone where messages get mixed up when repeated mouth to ear. Mike brings up Hanukkah and Mezuzah as examples of oral law. I counter with Mezuzah is in the written law.

"It is commanded to 'put the word upon your doors and gates,'" I say.

Pinner says, "Some people in Israel actually write Bible verses all over their doors."

I say, "That's an interesting interpretation. But I still feel that written law trumps oral law because written law cannot be changed while oral is easy to change." I am pretty sure we all disagree and have seven opinions amongst the three of us.

"Where do your parent's go to Shul?" asks Mike

"They don't they aren't very religious" I say. "I come from two generations of marrying out."

"What do you mean?" Pinner asks.

"My grandmother married a gentile, and so did my mother, I guess I did too, only he's converting. So, I guess I am three generations out," I say.

"Then how do you know you are a Jew?" Mike asks.

"That would be Don Nachman's fault," I say. The looks on both their faces demand an explanation.

"When I was about 21 or so, I worked for a Jewish man in Virginia. I was a customer service rep for his janitorial company. He was driving me around introducing me to his clients and showing me what to look for, and how to do my job. One day while driving on the Interstate, he started complaining about his partners, a white man, and a black woman, who hate him because he is Jewish. They always thought he was stealing because he is the bookkeeper and Jewish. I told him 'that is silly, no Christian could possibly hate Jews because in the Bible it says the Jews are G-ds chosen people, and he who blesses the Jews is blessed and he who curses the Jews is cursed.' He still insisted they hated him because he is Jewish. Then I said, 'Well my grandma is Jewish and people do not hate her because she is Jewish.'"

"All of a sudden, he slams on brakes in the middle of the Interstate and pulls into the middle median. I remember thinking, 'Oh snap, he's going to fire me, and throw me out of his car.'"

"Then, he turns to me, absolutely serious, he asks me, 'Which grandmother?'"

"'Which grandmother? What do you mean which grandmother?' I ask."

"'Your mother's mother or your father's mother?' he demands."

"'My grandmother. What does it matter which grandma?' I ask, thinking he is really weird to demand something I had not ever thought about."

"'It matters, which one?' he demands."

"'That would be my mother's mother, I hadn't thought of it that way,' I say to him as cars whiz past us on the Interstate. He starts the car again and finds a break to pull back into the fast lane."

"Then, he smugly tells me, 'You're Jewish!'"

"I am not Jewish, I only said my grandmother is Jewish, I am not."

"'Yeah, you're Jewish,' Mr. Nachman said."

"No, my grandmother is Jewish, I'm not Jewish. I do not know anything about Jewish. I do not speak Hebrew or anything. I have never been to a Temple. How can I be Jewish? I don't know anything about Jewish, other than what it says in the Bible. I am not Jewish, and I think you are insulting Jewish people. I don't know anything about it, so how can I be Jewish? They study things, and you are insulting Jewish people everywhere 'cause I don't know anything."

"'I think you're Jewish, but I am going to check with my Rabbi,' Nachman insisted."

"'You can think anything you want, and I don't care what your Rabbi says. I am not Jewish because I don't know anything about it.' The conversation ended once he said he was going to ask his Rabbi."

"I remembered my great-grandmother's warning to read the Bible for myself and not rely on what men said. I looked at Mr. Nachman and wondered how he can be a chosen people and still defer to some other man's opinion."

"The next morning when I came in to work, Mr. Nachman called me into his office and said, 'You're going to lunch with me today.' I worried all morning long, sure I was going to get fired from the only job I had lied to obtain. I desperately needed a summer job or I would not be able to continue college. Nobody was hiring summer help, so I decided to lie and pretend I would stay at any job I interviewed for, forever, instead of only for the summer. Don Nachman had hired me, and here I was going to get fired at lunch."

"Mr. Nachman took me to the oldest kosher deli in Virginia. I did not know what to order so he ordered 'something good' for me—my first pastrami sandwich. I wasn't allowed to have cheese on it, but it was mighty good. He explained the matrilineal lineage to determine Jewishness. I still wasn't convinced with his 'Here's a pastrami sandwich, now welcome to the tribe' approach. It wasn't until years later when my husband wanted to convert, that I gave a second thought about *my* being a Jew."

I look Mike and Daniel in the eyes, and say, "If you don't like me being Jewish, you can go take it up with Don Nachman and his Rabbi. They are in Norfolk, Virginia." Little do I know, the longstanding mayor of Ariel is Ron Nachman.

Mike leaves to deliver the Shabbat food to the widow and our K-9 handlers. Daniel leaves for his house. I am left alone in the kitchen to fix the tables for Shabbat, with Ari and Elchonon, the latest Yeshiva K-9 handlers. Ari helps a little, Elchonon mostly smokes cigarettes. White table cloths, and paper plates set at every chair. Candles in the corner for any women to light, we set out the wine, bread, and salads. I make up olive and pickle trays, check the cholent in the kitchen and the soup simmering on the stove. Then I leave the kitchen for home, to shower up. I'll feed the dogs after Shabbat dinner because I bring any leftover scraps or bones to add to the dogs' food.

Mike makes it back in time for Shabbat. I don't remember anything eventful about this particular Shabbat. Of course we are on "high alert," again.

Sometime after Shabbat, Mike gets word over the Mers telephone that all the dog handlers at Ozeri's have been arrested. The widow and her children have been forcibly removed from her home. A bulldozer levels the house her husband hand-build from clay and rocks. Few of her possessions are saved when the army plops her and her children down in an apartment in Ariel.

By the second day, I demand Mike drive me out to the hill to rescue the dogs that are simply left in the van. I doubt they have any water and surely they have no food. Mike refuses.

I plead the rest of the day how the army "surely isn't inhumane we have to get the dogs." I offer to pretend to be the Israeli SPCA—they do not have one. "How can those peacenik types go over to the Palestine Authority and scream and harass the IDF, yet I cannot go and save the lives of a bunch of trained dogs?"

Mike still refuses.

The next day, we go to Ariel and pick up our dog handlers at the jail. They are released without charges filed, as if nothing has ever happened. Then, finally we have permission to pick up the dogs. One of the guys drives the van back. I am riding with Mike. Elihav, the Peruvian head of village security is also on the trip. He thinks I have come to Israel to find a husband.

I let him know, "I already have a husband."

Then he speculates how I am "looking for some kind of adventure or maybe to have an affair."

"Yeah right, I need to go to Israel to cheat on my husband. If I want to cheat, I'll just cheat, I don't need to go to Israel to have an affair. Like there's no good-looking guys in Hollywood," I say.

Chapter 10
Mission from G-d

Feb 15, 2003 - Corporal Noam Bahagon, 20, of Elkana; Sergeant Tal Alexei Belitzky, 21, of Rishon Lezion; Staff-Sergeant Doron Cohen, 21, of Rishon Lezion; and Sergeant Itay Mizrahi, 20, of Be'er Sheva are killed when their tank drives over an explosive device weighing 100 kgs. while on patrol in the Gaza Strip. Hamas claims responsibility for the attack.

Feb 23, 2003 - Sergeant Doron Lev, 19, of Holon is shot and killed when a Palestinian sniper opens fire at an army position in the southern Gaza Strip. The PFLP claims responsibility for the attack.

www.jewishvirtuallibrary.org

At home in the evening, I feed and water my dog. I write in my journal late into the night. I have a space heater a few inches from my long John covered legs and a blanket around my shoulders.

All of a sudden, I hear screams of many of the guys outside my house. Donnie is screaming "Let us in! Ari's been hurt!" I can hear many more of the dog handler's voices. Something about someone is shot, or hit or something. I have no idea what has happened. Has someone been shot? Broken an arm or leg? What?

I jump up, grab my medical kit throw it on the bed, find a pair of rubber gloves, quickly tie a Hawaiian pareo around my hips, and swing the door open. I am not at all concerned about my ridiculous appearance in long Johns and a pareo. I am still tying the pareo in a knot when half a dozen K-9 handlers pour into my house. I try to sort out who is actually hurt. Everyone is on their feet so that is good, I think. I put on rubber gloves. Everyone is talking at once.

"What happened?" I say.

"Ari's been bit," someone says. The story comes out quickly from many mouths. "Elchonon almost got shot," someone else offers.

"Are you shot?" I question Elchonon.

"No."

Everyone is talking all at once. It is hard to get the whole story.

Finally, I swing my arms and say, "Who's hurt?" Everyone points to Ari who is cradling one hand. "Show me," I demand. Still, everyone is trying to explain what happened, and who is at fault.

I tell everyone to "shut up." I question Ari about what happened. He says he got bit by one of the dogs; everyone starts to interject exactly how he got bit. I again tell everyone to "shut up I don't care how he got bit, or whose fault it is."

I examine the wound and ask how long ago this happened—maybe five minutes. It is a couple of puncture wounds, teeth marks that aren't bleeding. I check his hand for movement, pain, or broken bones. Nothing is broken, and he has no real pain. I tell Ari to go into the bathroom and turn on the hottest water he can handle and press on the holes and "make them bleed" to flush out any germs from the dog's mouth. "The more you can get it to bleed, the better," I say.

While Ari is flushing out his wounds in the bathroom, I turn my attention to the crowd of dog handlers in my room. "Okay," I say, "What happened?" Everyone talks at once, pointing and talking about getting shot. It makes no sense.

Ari comes out of the bathroom, holding his injured hand in the other hand. I take a clean paper towel and dry it off then pull him over to the sink outside the bathroom and pour iodine over the puncture holes. Using a couple of four by fours, I bandage up his hand taping the gauze in place. I tell him, "You must keep an eye on it for any sign of infection. Most likely it will be fine, but keep an eye the hand." I give him extra four by fours and tape telling him if he can't put it on himself to come back and I will change his bandages. Tennessee volunteers to change it tomorrow.

Ari helps explain what happened. Elchonon and Ari had gone down to the kennels to feed the dogs, and take two of the dogs out for shmira duty. Ari had decided to use one of the bigger more aggressive dogs. He was attempting to clip him onto a training collar, when the dog twisted. In order to prevent the dog from running loose, Ari grabbed him. The dog bit Ari in the process. Elchonon saw this, and thought his friend was being mauled to death. He panicked and ran to the closest house, Donnie and Tennessee's. The entire time Elchonon was yelling "Achshav!" and other things in Hebrew and English.

Donnie, Tennessee, Canada and a couple of others in the house, heard the commotion and thought someone was being attacked by terrorists. Tennessee grabbed an Uzi and aimed it at the door. Donnie stood behind the door, waiting. Then, he swung it open fast, when Elchonon begun beating on the door. They all figured terrorists must be following whoever it was, so they waited for the terrorists to follow Elchonon into the house. When no terrorists were forthcoming, they got the story about Ari up at the kennels. Everyone then ran to the kennels to help Ari, who by this time, had subdued the 120 pound shepherd.

Now, everyone in my house is yelling at Elchonon. They are blaming him, either for leaving Ari, or that he is running around the village yelling "terrorist."

"I don't think "achshav" means terrorist," I say.

There is much more anger, yelling, and pointing at Elchonon. Everyone wants a bad guy, so they can have a good guy. Ari is the innocent good guy who got bit. Somebody has to be the bad guy. Since there is no Muslims around to blame, Elchonon is it. Everyone wants Elchonon to be the bad guy. "There is way too much testosterone and cowboy mentality in my room," I think.

"Elchonon did the right thing," I say to the many arguments from the guys. "According to all first aid laws, if you cannot help, your duty is to call 9-1-1. Since there is no 9-1-1, he did the next best thing, and went to where he knew he could get help. That is the right thing to do!"

They still insist he should have stayed and helped Ari, or he almost got shot by Tennessee, or it is all his fault.

"Tennessee is an Olympic shooter and hunter, he knows better than to shoot until he sees his target. Elchonon did the right thing. That dog is hard to handle. Elchonon couldn't do it by himself. He would only make the situation worse, and maybe become a victim himself. He got help. If you can't help, you get help—that's the rule. It doesn't matter whose fault it is. Ari's fine, nobody got shot, it worked out. No more buts. Who is on shmira?"

"I go on at two." Canada says.

"Can you start a little earlier?" I ask. Canada and another Yeshiva boy agree to cover the rest of Ari and Elchonon's shift. The guys leave.

* * *

The next morning, Mike asks me "Well why did you come to Israel?" He makes himself a cup of coffee.

In my best *Blues Brothers* imitation I say, "I'm on a mission from G-d." I am not sure he saw that movie, because he looks pretty puzzled. So I proceed with this story:

> Okay, here's how it is, there is this guy who is drowning, so he starts praying. He says all the Psalms and all the prayers he knows for G-d to save him. All of a sudden a man appears in a boat and throws a rope to the drowning man.
>
> "Quick grab the rope" the guy in the boat says.

"NO," the drowning man says. "I am praying to G-d and he is going to save me."

So the man in the boat leaves. The man keeps praying harder, he says every prayer he knows forwards and backwards as well as all the Psalms forwards and backwards for G-d to save him.

Then all of a sudden a man on the cliff overlooking the bay where the man is drowning throws a rope down to the drowning man. "Grab the rope and I will pull you up," he says.

The drowning man says "NO, G-d is going to save me because I believe in G-d and I am praying all these prayers." So the man on the cliff leaves.

Then the man starts to pray even harder. He says the entire Torah and all prayers he knows, and even some he doesn't know. He says the entire book of Psalms three times. Then a helicopter comes along, and the pilot throws a ladder down and says, "Quick, climb up the ladder and you will be saved."

The man again refuses because he says he's "praying and G-d will save him." The helicopter leaves. The man drowns.

He goes up to heaven and is told he cannot come into heaven because he doesn't believe in G-d. The man throws a hissy fit and demands to speak to G-d. G-d comes by and says he has to go to hell because he doesn't believe in Him.

The man says, "I prayed and prayed for You to help. I said the Amidah, the entire book of Psalms and the Torah. I did not lose my faith. I knew you would save me from drowning."

G-d says "I sent a boat, the man on the cliff and a helicopter, what more do you want from me?"

I look at Mike and say, "Just think of me as the guy in the boat."

* * *

Ari arrives at the kitchen with Elchonon and shows me something he has in a bag. Ari asks me if I have ever seen these.

I tell him, "the dogs love them as a chew treat."

Then Ari brings the pig's ear out of the sack.

"Don't put it on the table, put it away quick," Mike says.

"Why? Nobody's going to eat it, it is for the dogs," I say.

Ari slips the dried up pig's ear back into the paper sack.

I receive a phone call on my cell phone from DHL. The delivery service driver will not come to the village to deliver a package from America, no matter how many directions I give the man. He says he is scared to drive out into the West Bank, and definitely will not even try to drive into Tapuach.

"He must be a Muslim," I think. K'far Tapuach is one of the few places that wisely does not allow the cheap Muslim help to enter the village. If any person in Tapuach hires a Muslim, they are ostracized in the village, and the Muslim is escorted to the front gate. This is the main reason I always feel much safer once I return inside Tapuach's gates. At least there will not be a "friendly" Muslim working inside the fence. Friendly that is, until they decide to either blow themselves up, or open the back door and let someone else blow themselves up.

The driver will meet me in Ariel however. Tennessee agrees to go to Ariel with me.

I tell the driver I will be there around ten A.M. when the bus gets there. "There will be two of us, a male with an orange baseball cap, and a shorter female wearing American army camouflage pants."

I take care of the morning feedings, and then catch the bus into Ariel to get my care package. Donnie tags along. We wait in the median across from the Ariel bus stop—the one right before entering Ariel.

Finally, a minivan approaches and stops. A man hands me a package from my husband. The guy didn't even ask my name or a signature or anything. We stand in the median and watch him hang a u-ey. I tear the package open, hoping for some goodies. Yes! Snickers bars and M&M's surround a disposable camera and film. There is also a long letter, I quickly fold into my pocket for later. Donnie devours one of the Snickers bars in one inhalation, Tennessee saves his for later.

"You better hide yours from Donnie," I tease Tennessee.

We cross the street, step over the black and white checkered gutter-curb and start up the hill to Ariel, when I receive a phone call from David Ha'iveri asking if we can do a K-9 demonstration for some visitors this afternoon. Tennessee and Donnie agree to handle the bite dogs and I will demonstrate the tracking dogs. We turn around, cross the street, and head right back to Tapuach. We hitchhike back, like we always do.

While we are waiting to hitchhike or "tremp" as they say in Hebrew, we try to figure out the protocol. One does not rudely stick out one's thumb, but rather points to the ground at a 45 degree angle with their forefinger. Seems the person furthest forward is the next one to be picked up. We are next, but when a car approaches, some guy behind us jumps in front and snags our ride. It happens three more times.

"I thought we were next," Donnie says.

We discuss how we will ever get a ride with our American sensibilities. It's not that we are so polite, but compared to Middle Easterners, we are Emily Post reincarnated.

Next, we move far away from the group of people waiting to get rides to places with limited bus service. We backup about 50 yards from the group of trempers.

"The cars will see us first, and then we can get a ride," Donnie says. We hope to get a ride before the crowd which keeps jumping in front of us and stealing our rides. The three of us agree, this is not only a great idea, but probably the only way we will ever get in a car.

All of a sudden some guy, none of us had even seen, comes over to us, and scolds us to "get back with all the others." We look puzzled at the guy. After all who is he, and where did he come from? He explains to us, "You must stay with the Jews. If you separate yourselves, everyone will think you are Arabs." We sheepishly move back with the crowd.

* * *

Back in the village, Mike has set up a nice lunch spread for the visitors. I take my package back to my house.

The visitors arrive to the kitchen and introductions are made all around. The mother of the Bar Mitzvah boy asks me all kinds of questions about how I handle the dogs. She probably hasn't seen any non-paved roads or cites, maybe she's scared of trees. The village is primitive by New York standards. I tell her we have electricity and computers. And maybe she is one of those Jews related to a Holocaust survivor who is afraid of dogs. I tell her I grew up with dogs. She says the village is "so isolated." I tell her it's like camping. She is still not convinced.

Finally we go outside and start the dog demo. Tennessee, Donnie, and Moshe put on the sleeve and bite suit with a kaffiah, and show the visitors how the dogs can disarm a terrorist. Moshe has one of the K-9s bite the sleeve, then he swings the dog around with the dog hanging on by his teeth. It is quite impressive. Tennessee commands two dogs to attack Donnie who is wearing the bite suit. The dogs pull him to the ground.

I give the Bar Mitzvah boy a clean four by four gauze pad to stick under his shirt for the duration of the show. When the bite work is done, I give him a plastic baggie, and have him place the scent article in the bag. He gives it back to me. "Go about four or five houses down, and run around the corner and hide," I say.

He does exactly that.

"Are you ready to run?" I say to the visitors.

The group nervously nod their heads "yes."

"Okay follow me." I let Po-poki sniff the boy's scent article. He takes off in the direction of the hidden boy. We turn the corner about where the boy should have turned, but we cannot see him. He found an air conditioner to hide behind. The dog heads straight for the air conditioning unit, and around the side finds the crouching boy. Po-poki jumps up on his hind legs, and with his front paws, tags him. The young man laughs and pets Po-poki.

"You know, he is a Jewish dog."

"How can he be a Jewish dog?" the Bar Mitzvah boy asks.

"Because he's wearing a yarmulke," I say, pointing to the two inch brown circle on the top of the dog's head.

"But, is he circumcised?" asks the Bar Mitzvah boy.

"No, dogs don't have to be circumcised."

I think the mom liked how the dog is a "Jewish" dog. Everyone catches up to where we had made the "find" of the lost Bar Mitzvah boy.

I explain why we are training the other dogs for tracking, so they can catch terrorists, then disarm them with bites. We all head back to the kitchen for Mike's lunch.

Later, I go to do my laundry at the house where Jonathan is staying. Whoever owns the house is an absentee landlord from America. Only Jonathan can stay there, not the other bachelors. Jonathan is neat and clean and doesn't mess the house up like most of the young men do. Whoever owns the house has a big old hulking Maytag washer that was long ago converted to Israeli electricity. I really like the Maytag. Otherwise, I have to use the weird British front-loading washer. It takes almost all day to do one load. Maytag, forty-five minutes, and boom, laundry done, so much better.

Usually Jonathan is asleep when I do laundry, so I just go in the side door to the utility room. Today he is up, so we talk some. He tells me that the house is owned by an American Rabbi. "He is famous. He lives in California like you." He tells me the name of the Rabbi.

"Never heard of him," I say.

Then he shows me a book the Rabbi wrote, *Surfing Rabbi*.

"I know "Surfing Rabbi!" I say.

"Really?"

"Yeah, he goes to my Shul! Who knew? Here I am using Surfing Rabbi's washer."

Jonathan gives me Surfing Rabbi's book and I take it home to read. "Just bring it back when you are finished with it."

"Is he a Rabbi first, then he decided to surf? Or is he a surfer, and decided to get more religious?" I ask. Jonathan doesn't know.

I take my wet clothes back to my house and put them on the white metal Israeli drying rack. Since it is sunny out, I leave the rack outside in the sun.

Shabbat comes and Mike asks me "Don't you go to Chabad?"

"Yes."

"Well these two young men are from New York, and they know all about the Chabad in Marina Del Rey."

"Really?"

"We heard about it in New York," one says.

"Really? You heard about what happened and how it closed? All the way in New York?" I say.

"Oh yes. It is a big mess, a big balagan," one says.

The other chimes in, "The biggest scandal ever."

I look at Mike and say something to the effect that "You know that's where I'd be." I am not sure he really believed that I went to the Marina Del Rey Shul. During the conversation with the Yeshiva boys it becomes clear that I know Rabbi Shmuelik Naparstek and attend regularly. All three of us do not want to be guilty of lashon hora or evil tongue, so we abruptly stop talking about it. I still wonder what actually did happen.

"I thought you went to the Kabbalah Centre," Mike says.

"I told you, I did go there, but we stopped going because we did not like them sucking up to celebrities and other rich people. They treated some poorer Jews badly, so we simply quit one day right before High Holidays. We did not have anywhere to go. Pretty much it was the end of Judaism for the both of us. We'd had it. Then we got a post card from the Chabad saying services are free. We never really liked the idea of having to 'pay to pray.' If people tithed, they wouldn't have to do that.

Anyway, Chabad appealed to us. When we met Shmuelik and the other Rabbis and we liked them. They treated us like equals."

I think back on meeting Shmuelik, Leah and his family. My husband and I felt so honored and proud to be invited to his Shabbat table. Shmuelik is one of those rare individuals who has the ability to explain complex Jewish principals in such a way that the lowest of the low (like me) can understand; and he can just as easily relate to high-level Torah scholars, all the while keeping his own prayers in order.

My tenth grade teacher used to say that scientists are not good at their work unless they can explain their concepts to the street-level man. "When you can do that, you are a master in your field," he used to say.

"I sure hope they straighten out that trouble in Marina Del Rey," I say.

"Baruch HaShem."

Every Shabbat, we have to go on high alert around the village. The Muslims try to attack villages, or throw stones—which is more like pushing boulders off cliffs onto oncoming cars. They do all manner of evil things trying to catch Jews when they are vulnerable on Shabbat or any Jewish holiday. Our guarding cannot take a break for the Sabbath. Since we are trying to "save lives" our guard work is sanctioned by the Rabbis.

Tennessee and I are on guard duty early this Shabbat morning. We round a corner to the desolate side of the village. All of a sudden a man drops a magazine and runs off. The sun is barely peaking over the mountains.

"Something's not right."

Chicken skin crawls up my back to my neck. We look sideways at each other, then to where the magazine lay. We haven't broken our pace, but we do shift our direction slightly so as to investigate the magazine.

"Did he have on tzitzit?"

"I don't think so," Tennessee says.

"Did he have a yarmulke?"

"I'm not sure."

"What is he doing out so early?"

"Something's not right."

We continue to walk toward where the man dropped the magazine. We get to the magazine, and it is a fashion magazine!

"This is a religious village, why is he reading a fashion magazine, on Shabbat?"

"Why is he reading a fashion magazine at all?" Tennessee says.

"But it is Shabbat, the only thing he should be reading is the Torah," I say.

"Something's not right, and where did he go?"

"I'm gonna go get my dog. Don't let anyone touch that magazine." I point to the magazine for emphasis. "That's the scent article, don't let anyone touch it, I'll be right back." I say. I trot away toward the kennels. I get rid of the Malinois and jog over to my house. I grab Po-poki, his harness, and a tracking line. Maybe fifteen minutes pass since I ran to get Po-poki and the tracking equipment. Tennessee has called Canada and Donnie on the radio, for backup while I was gone.

Canada is out walking the road to the summit with Tarzan, one of the German Shepherds. Canada often walks down to the checkpoint and tells the shepherd to bark at the Muslims, while the IDF checks them for explosives. Today, Canada is accompanied by Donnie on his barking mission.

It is only Tennessee and me. I harness the dog up, and scent him on the magazine. He takes off toward the fence. We come to a hole in the fence. We stop. We inspect the hole.

"It's been cut," I say.

"Naw, it's old. Look, it has rust on the cut."

"Yeah, you're right. But where'd he go? Dog says he went this way."

"I'm not sure we should go outside the fence."

"What do you think we should do?" Po-poki pulls on the leash which I have choked up to three feet between us.

"The army could shoot us on accident," Tennessee says.

"That or the terrorist, but this is where he went."

After more pro and con discussion, we decide to venture outside the fence. Tennessee holds the barbed wire apart for me to get through. The dog jumps through the hole. I hold the barbed wire apart so Tennessee can duck through the hole.

Po-poki tracks to an area where the grass is mashed down, as if someone was lying down, watching. We come to a cliff that leads down to the highway. Then the trail goes cold. Whoever it was escaped down the hill and most likely caught a ride with a waiting car. Both of us are disappointed that we did not catch a terrorist.

We trudge up the hill and back inside the fence. We take the magazine to the kitchen. I take Po-poki home. We meet again at the kitchen, and tell Mike what happened. He calls village security, and the IDF at the front gate, and tells them what happened. Tennessee and I head out to finish our shmira duty. Mike and the Yeshiva boys head over to Shul.

Chapter 11
Translations

Mar 5, 2003 - Seventeen people are killed and 53 wounded in a suicide bombing of an Egged bus #37 on Moriah Blvd. in the Carmel section of Haifa, en route to Haifa University. Hamas claims responsibility for the attack. The victims: Maryam Atar, 27, of Haifa; Smadar Firstater, 16, of Haifa; Kamar Abu Hamed, 12, of Daliat al-Carmel; Daniel Haroush, 16, of Safed; Mordechai Hershko, 41, of Haifa; Tom Hershko, 15, of Haifa; Meital Katav, 20, of Haifa; Elizabeta Katzman, 16, of Haifa; Tal Kerman, 17, of Haifa; Staff-Sergeant Eliyahu Laham, 22, of Haifa; Abigail Litle, 14, of Haifa; Yuval Mendelevitch, 13, of Haifa; Staff-Sergeant Be'eri Oved, 21, of Rosh Pina; Mark Takash, 54, of Haifa; Assaf Tzur (Zolinger), 17, of Haifa. Anatoly Biryakov, 20, of Haifa, died of his injuries on March 8. Moran

Shushan, 20, of Haifa, died of her injuries on March 11.

www.jewishvirtuallibrary.org

On the far side of the village is a Torah manufacturer. They take goatskins, tan them, and then stretch them on metal frames to dry out. Once completely dry, they sand off any hair or imperfections, making a perfectly smooth surface for writing Torah letters. When the sanding part is done, they cut the skins to one of two sizes using a Plexiglas pattern. Maybe it is for two different sized Torahs depending on the size of the goat. There is lots of extra goatskin from around the edges of the square patterns. Goats do not come square shaped. All the remnants of goatskins are tossed in the trash. I ask the guy doing all the work if I can have the scraps of goatskin. He is more than happy to give them to me.

I think they are soaked in lime or something. So, I re-soak the hard goatskins in warm water to remove the lime. Then I roll the scraps up into a little roll, as tight as I can, and tie a knot. I leave them to then dry on my windowsill. They are about five inches long and rolled like a crescent roll, fat around the middle and narrower on the ends, somewhat brownish-grayish in color.

Once dry, they make great chew toy treats for the dogs. They do not have any weird poisonous chemicals like the Chinese leather chews have, and it cleans the dog's teeth. I usually have a dozen or so drying on my windowsills. Jonathan tells me he thinks they are dead birds I have killed, and left on the windowsill as some kind of warning. It's weird how simple things can be misunderstood.

Vegan Josh and Big-Hair Josh have both left us. Mike had tried to accommodate Vegan Josh by buying some Israeli vegan things, but they taste completely nasty.

Mike always says "Mmmm Mmm" and brings the horrible vegan food out of the oven trying to get all of us to like it. Vegan Josh is the only one who can stand it. After tasting some of the disgusting vegan things, the rest of us look in amazement and horror that anyone can eat it at all. Pita with hummus is just fine for the rest of us. Never mind the "official" vegan thing.

The Ben Boys, Laeb, and Shaul have show up with their father Ben. They bring with them a couple of tiny mutts they found wandering in Jerusalem. They have no money for dog food, so you guessed it. They are constantly begging for dog food, and who can say no?

Yesterday I was walking through the village and I saw a woman frantically trying to get her dog over the railing of her balcony. She had chained the German Shepherd on her balcony, and the dog had jumped over the railing. Pretty much, the dog was hanging itself.

She is scared of the dog, which is such a sweet dog. The dog does not have a mean bone in it. I run over to unclip the chain. Since I always carry a tracking leash on my belt, I clip the dog onto my leash, and bring it through her house back onto the balcony. I try to tell her it is not necessary to chain the dog in addition to leaving it on the balcony; but her English is not so good. I think it might be her husband's dog.

I know barely a few phrases in Hebrew, cannot hold a conversation, and am basically illiterate. Since all the Shabbat services are in Hebrew with no translations in the books, Saturday morning services are meaningless for me. Therefore, I take Saturday morning shmira so as to allow others, who do understand Hebrew, to attend service. The guys rotate who will guard with me. Lucky for me, I usually have an armed guy. Mike still has not arranged for me to qualify at the army gun range.

Today's flanker is Yossi. He's studying computers at Ariel University. We are chatting, walking, and enjoying the beautiful clear crisp Shabbat morning. Tiny clouds of cold condensation surround our heads as we walk near the fence. As we walk the line, we separate ourselves a slight distance.

Briefly, I review the commands for the dog I am using. I have one of the Czech dogs on lead.

I had long ago made up cheat sheets with each dog's commands, because some were originally trained in German, Czech, Hungarian, Bulgarian, Austrian or Russian. While the commands are close, the words are not quite all the same. Even though the dog team is trying to switch over to exclusively Hebrew, the dogs respond best in their original language of learning.

We stop at one of the many protected lookout points that provide strategic views of the surrounding area. We still chat aimlessly. Things haven't been hairy lately, even though Mike always says we are on "high alert." Sometimes, I think he completely exaggerates. We do our duty, look in all directions, and then continue our shmira perimeter walk.

Canada is at the other end of the village. Over the radio, he says he might walk a dog down to the summit in a few minutes. Probably for another of his bark fests. Due to static, we end our conversation with Canada and continue on our way. The K-9 heels perfectly. "Must have been a patrol dog in Czechoslovakia," I think to myself.

A shot rings out. "Where'd that come from?" I say.

"My leg! I'm hit in the leg," Yossi says.

The dog goes nuts at the sound of the gunshot. He is now barking and pulling. He wants to go after the shooter. I cannot let him go because it could be an ambush to get the dog. My flanker is down so I have no protection, to let the dog chase a bad guy.

"Are you okay?" I am now screaming, reaching into my pocket for the handheld radio. I worry about what I say over the radio because it is obvious we are being monitored, but I have to get help. "Man down! We got a man down, Canada are you there? Canada? Anybody? Mayday! We need help up here at the water tower. We're at the migdol mayim."

I turn around to where Yossi is, slightly up the hill from me. He is leaning back seated. I run the few yards up to where he is, all the while screaming into the radio. I am not getting any answer from anyone. Shit, Canada might be out of range, if he left for the summit! I think. "Are you okay?" I scream.

"Ken, I am hit in the leg!" Yossi says.

I think, femoral artery, three minutes to bleed out. I reach for the fanny pack that I typically have with me and realize I was too lazy this morning and did not put it on. "Shit! Are you okay?" I frantically search every pocket of my BDU's for tampons, which I always carry specifically for bullet holes. I realize I do not have any. "Dammit, I don't have anything!"

Sam's Emergency First Responder class flashes in my mind. I see Sam in my mind's eye explaining how if you are somewhere and do not have a CPR mask, you can use a garbage bag. I yell at the dog to down stay in Hawaiian,

Hebrew then Czech. The dog downs. I desperately search for a substitute bandage. I look at the leash thinking I can make a tourniquet out of the leash . . . shoelaces . . . three minutes . . . femoral artery.

"Help, we need help here migdol mayim. Yossi's been shot. Mayday! Mayday!" I am screaming into the radio. To hell with the Palestinians, I need help. Trying to come up with a solution to the bandage problem, I strip off my white long sleeved T-shirt, with the cool retro 45-disc centerpiece logo. "Let me see your leg!"

Canada comes over the radio. He says he is on the way.

"Hurry, you are the only help! Hurry! Yossi's been shot migdol mayim!" It is so static that I don't know if he heard me.

Yossi shows me his ankle. That is where he has been hit, in the ankle. Well, I guess technically it is the leg, but the leg? I am still running on adrenalin. I demand to see the exit wound. He doesn't want to take off his shoe. I demand him to take it off. He refuses.

"There is no time for this! If you are modest, or you have a hole in your sock, or stinky feet. Just take your shoe off!"

I see the exit wound and it is small and clean, which is good. The ammunition must have been old, or it would have made a bigger exit wound. I put my right leg out like a base for holding a cheerleader in a pyramid. "Here.

Put your foot right here on my leg." I take my shirt and use it as a bandage with the arms becoming the ties to the bandage I cross them over the top of his foot, under his arch, and behind his ankle. Then I tie a knot. This at least stabilizes the ankle. He is not bleeding much; it is only oozing very slowly. Tying the T-shirt on the foot and ankle is pretty much all I can do. He's awake and conscious, and probably has a slower heartbeat and respiration than me.

Finally, Canada arrives, his mini peyos sticking out straight sideways from his head. He is panting having run from more than half way down the summit, across the village, and up to the Migdol Mayim, a total of about two to three miles, uphill the entire way.

He has not caught his breath, when I tell him to go to the Shul and get Mike. He doesn't know which Shul Mike goes to. I tell him "Just go to the closest one, the one with the navy blue Ten Commandments on the outside." It is still at least a quarter of a mile away. "Tell them Yossi's been shot, and you need some help, at the migdol mayim." He doesn't want to interrupt the service and complains he doesn't speak Hebrew. "It doesn't matter, this is life threatening. You can interrupt. Someone will speak English, just go. Go!" I yell, pushing him down the hill.

In short order, Mike arrives and tells me how he heard on the radio that someone got shot. Mike goes to the same Shul as Yossi's parents. Mike explains what came over the radio was that the "girl dog handler had shot the boy dog handler." He says, "Yossi's parents are on the way."

"Oh my G-d! I did not shoot Yossi!" I look around and see two extremely worried looking parents barreling our way; her full flowered skirt, and his long peyos flying behind. I look to see if they are armed. I do not see a gun, but you never know, the holster could be in back. Wait, the dad has an Uzi slung over his shoulder. For a brief moment, I think of running away.

I again flash back to Sam's class and how if you ever have to do CPR on an infant, the parents will often demand to hold the baby, even though the baby is clearly dead. "Don't ever tell the parents that the child is dead, just give them the child to hold. They will blame you, and often get violent," Sam said.

"You have to tell them that I did not shoot him," I demand of Mike, my eyes wide with horror.

The village's Emergency First Responders arrive with first aid packs. They administer an IV and get Yossi on a stretcher.

I run over to the mom and dad and scream, "I did not shoot him! I did not shoot him!" Then I run to put the dog away in the kennels.

When I get back, Pinner is here. Pinner starts telling jokes. I think it's a British thing. I have completely lost my sense of humor and snarl at him. Village security arrives and takes a report, since whoever did it is long gone, not much can be done.

At lunch, we debrief. Mike tells his version of what happened. He was sitting in Shul when over the radio comes word that a girl had shot someone. Yossi's parents asked, "who got shot?" Mike in ever the understatement says, "Oh, that would be your son."

Ramon asks, "What did you use for a bandage?"

"I took off my shirt and used that," I say.

"Ooooooo," all the guys say, as if it is some kind of sexual thing.

"I was wearing five shirts! I still had four shirts on, so what's the big deal?" I demand of the guys, looking at them through fiery eyes.

They all get suddenly pin drop quiet.

Later in the week, Mike gives me an enameled symbolic "Jewish Legion" pin and a Letter of Commendation. The rest of the guys stand and salute me in a goofy ceremony.

Mike brings out some left over vegan things, and cheese pizza. "Mmmm mmmm," Mike says.

Everyone groans.

Chapter 12
The Girlfriend

March 7, 2003 - Rabbi Eli Horowitz, 52, and his wife Dina, 50, of Kiryat Arba, are killed and five wounded Friday night by armed terrorists disguised as Jewish worshippers who infiltrated Kiryat Arba, enter their home and murder them while they are celebrating the Sabbath. Hamas claims responsibility for the attack.

Mar 10, 2003 - Staff-Sergeant Tomer Ron, 20, of Moshav Moledet, is killed and four soldiers are wounded, one seriously, in Hebron, on the road between the Cave of the Patriarchs and Kiryat Arba, when Palestinian terrorists open fire on a foot patrol. Two organizations - Hamas and Ahmed Jibril's Popular Front General Command claim responsibility for the attack.

www.jewishvirtuallibrary.org

Craig and Shimon decide to rent the house next to Yocheved's house. The house is owned by her friend in Texas, who returned to America after a couple of trial years in Israel. Yocheved handles the rental finances for her friend. Craig is making aliyah and Shimon is thinking about it. They gather their furniture, beds, possessions and try to make their bachelor pad manly.

Shimon, who is from Florida, has left on yet another of his Sar-El missions at the army base. He packs parachutes or does any number of menial tasks to help the IDF.

This night, Craig is home alone. He is trying to pass a couple of kidney stones, which the entire west side of the village is sympathetically aware of, when the alarm goes out that a dog has been shot.

Yoni is back temporarily, and we both run toward the shooting. It is not one of our K-9's, but the dog is in really bad shape. It is a villager's dog, shot by another villager during a dogfight. "That's a hell of a way to break up a dog fight," I mumble to Yoni.

Yoni and I both kneel to inspect the wounds. The dog has lost a lot of blood. He doesn't even care that strangers are checking him. I am fully prepared to make a makeshift muzzle out of a leash, but it's not even necessary. The mutt's eyes are glazed over and he is panting heavily. We roll him over and inspect the other side, the exit wounds. A crowd gathers around. The owner is there but speaks no English. The shooter has wisely left. The only ones who speak English are Yoni and me.

It appears the three entrance and exit wounds have gone through most vital organs. The dog is clearly in shock. It really doesn't look good. Yoni is yammering to everyone in Hebrew. They listen because he is the dog trainer for the security dogs. He says the dog needs to go to the vet immediately and get on an IV to save it. The owner doesn't have any money.

I tell Yoni it is cruel to leave an animal suffering. "I don't think the dog will make it to the morning, but sometimes animals have remarkable healing ability. If it makes it 24 hours then it will live, but it will be suffering the whole time. And, it might not make it. It's a tossup call," I say.

Craig comes out of his house and is clearly upset by the whole scene. He doesn't understand much more Hebrew than me. Even though he has no money, having recently spent it all to rent the house, he demands to pay the vet bill. Nobody believes him. Craig kneels down with me and insists the dog will live because one of his wounds is pulsing with each heartbeat.

I tell him a rhythmical pulsing wound is not a sign of recovery, but rather "a sign of blood loss." Craig is almost hysterical, wanting to save the dog. Even when I hold his shoulders and look directly into his eyes and say, "We cannot let him suffer;" he still insists we let the dog live.

Yoni and I have a discussion about where to shoot the dog to kill it the quickest. We do not agree. He says it is the temple like a human's temple on the side of the dog's head. I say he has to hit the 'brain stem' which I think is where the spine joins the head. We continue to argue about where to shoot the dog with Craig screaming and pleading in the background. We ignore him. The owner racks his gun.

I look at Yoni and say, "Can someone else shoot the dog, so the owner doesn't have to shoot his own dog?" I dare not grab the gun myself, because, well, in this man's country, machismo is an understatement.

The man shoots his dog.

Craig is crying, pleading, and in so much pain, he calls us a stream of vile names. Then, finally, thankfully, he goes inside. A couple of men help throw the dog into the dumpster. The crowd goes home.

Yoni and I go back to the kitchen and get coffee. I show him some of my training books. We discuss different training methods. Donnie and Tennessee come into the kitchen. They look over our shoulders at the binder filled with training records and newspaper articles. I point to a *Jewish Journal* article about the victims of terrorism, which has a picture of Danielle Sheffi, a toddler who was shot by terrorists.

"This completely tore me up. The Palestinians wrote they 'killed a female settler.' A female settler! That is what they called her! She's a baby!"

"I remember that. It's why I came here, too," Donnie says.

Donnie and Tennessee leave for shmira. Yoni leaves, and I go home.

* * *

Later in the week, Shimon returns with a girlfriend in tow. This doesn't go over too well. Sex outside of marriage is frowned upon in this highly religious community. The girl is clearly Secular, being from Tel Aviv.

Shimon tells me she had told him she wants to "be more religious." I keep my thoughts to myself. However, I highly doubt a feisty young woman from a completely Secular background would all of a sudden want to dress, act, and be Orthodox, most especially without any kind of religious study. Stranger things have happened, you never know. I don't believe it. Perhaps, if she had some kind of terrible accident, coming close to death, maybe, but, really? Seriously? She all of a sudden wants to be religious? Naw, I'm just not buying it.

She wears a long skirt, but misses the whole modesty thing by matching it up with a skin-tight sleeveless T-shirt. Then, over the next week, she shows up after Shabbat has been officially declared, IN A CAR! The Orthodox have ruled that the spark plugs are creating a spark or a fire and so it is against the rules to drive on Shabbat. Throughout Israel, the only people who drive on the Sabbath are Gentiles, Emergency Personnel, or the Secular.

If it weren't for the IDF at the front gate, she would never be allowed into the village after Shabbat started. The reason the IDF let her in at all is because most of them are Secular Jews from other parts of Israel. This is their once a year assignment, in the far reaches of Israel's outback. They are mostly clueless about Orthodox religious observance.

Canada even has an ongoing joke about the middle-aged front gate IDF soldiers, still wearing their old army uniforms. "I'm too chubby for my bulletproof vest," Canada jokes in his best imitation Israeli accent.

Unlike my bulletproof vest, which is so huge, and the neck hangs so low I can get shot "center mass" through the neck hole, some of the men's vests can barely close.

In fact, Shimon's girlfriend's behavior endangers my reputation. One Rabbi's wife, don't ask me which one, ends up yelling at Mike about his dog handlers and especially his female dog handlers. The Rebbetzin assumes Shimon's girlfriend is also a dog handler, and says she is immodest and immoral. The girlfriend obviously hasn't gone to mikveh, and is sleeping with Shimon. Plus, she is dressed immodestly. In addition she is driving on Shabbat!

Mike tries to explain that she is not part of the dog team. Then, the Rabbi's wife starts to complain about the "other female dog handler," whom she says is also "immodest for wearing pants." That would be me. Poor Mike is left to defend me on this one.

He later warns Shimon about his girlfriend driving on Shabbat. He says the next time she shows up at the gate after Shabbat starts, she will be turned away regardless of how dangerous the road may be for her. I think something is also said about the sleepovers. It does not concern me, so I don't pay too much attention. For Shimon, his past would soon end this entire problem.

Sarah has invited me for Shabbat. She is the woman whose dog I helped get off her balcony railing—the shepherd that almost got hung. Most of the Yeshiva boys usually call around and kind of invite themselves to people's homes. It is the Israeli way. However, I find it completely uncomfortable to invite myself to someone's home. So this is my first invite. She is Chabad, but doesn't speak very good English. I make a mental note to bring an English-Hebrew dictionary. She said her husband is a Rabbi. I look forward to this all week long.

Finally, Shabbat arrives and I go over to her house right after dark. I am wearing BDU's as I have shmira afterwards. I put on a clean white blouse for the occasion and bring her children some light sticks to play with. I am not sure they can light them on Shabbat. I will have to explain to wait until after Shabbat. The dictionary is in my side pocket.

Sarah is excited to see me. The kids are too. They must not have many visitors, because the three kids just stare at me. Maybe because I am wearing pants. Yocheved's girl, Chaiki, told me one Shabbat, when I was not doing guard duty, and had on a Hawaiian pareo instead of pants, that I "now look like a girl." I remember thinking at the time, with my big butt, I always look like a girl.

I worry if I am influencing this Rabbi's children negatively by wearing pants. I have no way of explaining, because his English is as bad as my Hebrew. Throughout the dinner we pass the dictionary back and forth trying to talk to each other. We all know the same prayers, blessings, and songs, so that part goes well. It is only the dinner conversation that is sort of odd, disjointed, and at times funny trying to mime things.

Sarah has a lovely white table cloth and candles on the table, lighting up the precious wine and challah. The meal is simple, a clear broth soup with a chicken leg in everyone's bowl. I notice the mother does not have a chicken leg. I, however, as the guest, do. I am not fond of chicken legs, in fact I hate them. Here the Rebbetzin is giving me, the guest, her expensive piece of chicken. She goes without. I want to tell her I am a vegetarian and for her to take the chicken leg, but it is impossible and it would be rude. So I, as graciously as I can, accept the chicken leg, and heartily eat it with compliments.

She shows me an electric picture with a waterfall, her husband Mordechai had given her for their anniversary. She adores it. It is her favorite new modern thing in her house. I tell them I go to Chabad in Marina Del Rey. They do not know where that is. He has however, heard of California. Therefore, I go to Chabad in California.

"Ahhh, Cali-forn-nyia, Chabad Cali-forn-nyia," the Rabbi says.

The whole family smiles and says, "Cali-forn-nyia."

Rabbi Mordechai tells me he is only a small Rabbi. He uses his forefinger and thumb to make a sign of little. I am not quite sure what this means.

After dinner he shows me some mezuzah he makes. I am completely mesmerized. I tell him he is an artist. He doesn't know the word so I look up the word artist. He again says small and makes the hand signal for small. Maybe he means small because mezuzah is small. Small, compared to a Torah scroll.

It is not every day one can meet a mezuzah scribe. I tell him I want to buy some mezuzah from him. I am excited to have a mezuzah hanging in my house that I know who actually wrote it.

Sarah clears the dishes from dinner and brings out some tea and cookies for dessert. I give each child a light stick. Mordechai takes one and mimes to eat it. He thinks it is a dessert or a candy. I say "No! No LO! LO! Not for eat" I cannot explain it is a light, something fun for the kids to play with. I am horrified he might try to eat the light stick and get poisoned. I think, for sure this will get me a special place in hell for killing a loving husband, father, Rabbi, and mezuzah writer. They invite me for Shabbat, and I poison the dad. Oh, great.

So, I grab the light stick out of his hand and open the package and break the chemical to make it glow. The kid's eyes light up. I am not exactly sure if it is against the rules about kindling a fire on Shabbat but am pretty sure it is. I am embarrassed because I have come into his house, a Rabbi's house, and broken a serious commandment. And I did it in front of his impressionable children. I should have thought this lightstick thing through. I did say wait until after Shabbat to use it. Even though one can break every commandment to save a life, which is why I make the light stick glow; it is no consolation. I feel horrible.

* * *

The next week, Shimon and Craig are fighting. I don't think it ever came to blows, but one or the other of them moved out and moved in with Ramon and Yishai at the other end of the village. Yup, they are no longer friends.

The wanna be Orthodox girlfriend has scarcely fallen out of love with Shimon, when she just as quickly falls in love with Craig. I especially am not buying the whole Orthodox thing now. What kind of girl does that to a guy's best friend? I think many of us figured out the girl's plan. Shimon is still legally married. Craig is not.

Shimon says he can't say anything to Craig. "Craig thinks he is in love."

"Why do these Israelis think getting to America is all that?" I ask out loud. "Man, it is so sad, for Craig, to be used like that. Can't someone warn him?"

"I can't say anything to him. He thinks I am jealous," Shimon says. .

Mike only says, "Craig is a big boy."

Within the next month, Craig and the girlfriend leave for America. They get married. During the honeymoon, the girl simply takes off for parts unknown, her new marriage license/green card securely in hand. Even Shimon feels bad for Craig.

Chapter 13
The Goat Run

Mar 12, 2003 - Staff-Sergeant Assaf Moshe Fuchs, 21, of Kibbutz Gvat is killed and another soldier wounded Wednesday morning in an exchange of fire with wanted terrorists from the Islamic Jihad in the West Bank village of Saida, near Tulkarm.

Mar 18, 2003 - Sergeant-Major (reserves) Ami Cohen, 27, of Netanya is killed and another soldier wounded south of Bethlehem when Palestinians open fire during a search for wanted terrorists.

www.jewishvirtuallibrary.org

Yesterday, I had to move houses again, because Emmanuel may be coming back from Russia. I move most of my things to the new location, and figure I will wait until nightfall to move the Uzi I found under Emmanuel's bed. I've taken to calling the Uzi "Betty." I dare not get caught with this unauthorized gun or it's that seven-year prison thing. I wrap Betty in a towel and shove her into my dog crate. The minute it gets dark, I lug the dog crate with my secret over to my new house. I make it over without incident. I clean up yet another house. Bachelors, once again, were the previous ones who lived here. I hide Betty under my pillow.

Today, Mike wants to organize a trip to Masada but truly, I do not want to go there. "I don't want any of the vibes of losers," I say to Mike.

He says "They did not lose. They committed suicide."

"And, why did they commit suicide? Because they were losing!"

"It is more complicated than that. They're not losers," Mike says.

"Well, did they win?" I demand.

"Not exactly."

"Look, they either won or they lost. Committing suicide doesn't seem like a winning strategy. I wanna go somewhere where Jews kicked ass, like Jericho. I like winners. I wanna see the walls Joshua knocked down."

"You can't go there," Mike says.

"Whadda ya mean, you can't go there? Isn't it in Israel?"

"It's controlled by the Palestinians and they will kill you."

"Why do they get all the cool sites? They got the Temple Mount. They stole Bethlehem. Who gave them Jericho? Who are these creeps running around Israel saying mine, mine, mine? They're not even Jews. I want to see Jericho, but nooooooo; I have to go see some loser site. And, I am supposed to be happy about it. That just ain't right."

"Okay, forget it, we're going to Jerusalem," Mike says.

So, a group of us head to Jerusalem. He is going to drop us off, then designate a pick up point for later. We actually have two vans full of people. We say the traveler's prayer as we leave K'far Tapuach. I am sure it is being recited in the other vehicle as well. We pull out onto the main highway to Jerusalem.

I space out and wait for the first glimpse of Jerusalem to come into focus, a golden light shimmering from buildings tiled in gold Jerusalem stone. The rocky hillsides on the way are made up of strange white rocks that resemble skulls and bones sticking out of dirt. My mind wanders to all the Bible stories, all the wars, and fighting that happened over this tiny piece of real estate. G-d Himself even said, it is His land, and He gave it to the Jews. Nobody listens to that. Like taggers who spray paint buildings they will never own, people still fight over what is not theirs.

The motor drones on as we approach Jerusalem.

Mike tells us what corner to meet at 6:00 P.M. We joyfully jump out of the vans. I am hoping to go shopping, but know the guys will not want to shop. Right now, I hang with Canada, Donnie, and Tennessee. We wander the streets. Tennessee and Donnie want to go to the Temple Institute because they like Rabbi Chaim Richman. Canada and I never heard of this place or Rabbi, but it sounds good, so that is where we head off to.

Tennessee and Donnie aren't Jews and they aren't Christians. They are Bnei Noach, sons of Noah. They tell me of the Seven Laws of Noah. I really don't understand why they need seven more laws beyond the Ten Commandments. In fact, I really don't get the concept at all.

We tour the Temple Institute museum. It has re-made artifacts waiting for Temple service when the third Temple is rebuilt, or magically falls out of the sky. Solid gold candlesticks, bread plates, and other gold objects on display behind glass, await the right moment.

"I have heard there are children born who are raised in special rooms where their feet do not ever touch the ground, so they will be purified and ready for Temple service," I say.

"Really?" Canada says.

"Yeah, I am not exactly sure why and all that, but they are Cohens and special," I say.

Rabbi Richman is not around. We finish with the tour and leave.

We all decide to visit the Wall which is right below us. We descend the steep stairs down to the Western Wall of Solomon's Temple.

Tourists mingle with Secular and Orthodox Jews. We all wait in line to have bags X-rayed and go through security. We joke and talk while we wait. None of us has any knives, because Mike warned us not to carry knives if we plan to go to the Western Wall. Our group has now increased as the rest of the two vehicles manage to catch up to us four. We split into two lines and begin the process of going through security. Finally, we throw our backpacks onto the X-ray belts. "No," we all say to the security guards. "We do not have any knives." Those with guns, show their permits.

Today, I am wearing black BDU's and a black sweater with a green army style jacket. The security girl wants to know what is the orange coiled up webbing thing clipped onto my belt.

"It's a dog leash," I say.

"Is it religious?" she asks. She is clearly giving me extra scrutiny. Most of the guys are waiting for me.

At first, I do not comprehend her question because she asks me in Hebrew. Then, when she finally asks me in English, I still don't understand because it is such a weird question. So, I repeat her question, trying to grasp it. "Is it religious?" I furrow my brows trying desperately to figure out this bizarre line of questioning. I think to myself, "Does she really think a dog leash is some kind of religious icon, like prayer beads, or something?" She stands patiently, professional, emotionless, waiting for my answer. I look at Tennessee who is behind me. Okay, the devil takes over my mind, I can't resist.

"Yes!" I say. "You must pray to the dog leash." I stretch out three feet of leash and hold it up to her face.

Tennessee is trying not to laugh, but his eyes give him away. He even kicks me and tells me to shut up and be serious under his breath. "Stop it, you're gonna get us in trouble," he says.

We finally make it through the checkpoint and go to the Wall. All the guys go to the men's section, and I head over to the women's section. Some pray and we all put notes in the Wall. Tiny birds have made nests in crevices between the sandy gold colored stones of the Wall, mostly high up in the women's section. I watch them fly back and forth. Here and there, green plants grow in those very same cracks, grouted only with the tears of centuries of Jews.

Everyone takes off in different directions. Donnie and Canada go off somewhere, so Tennessee and I are buddies for the day. We decide to go to the shops next to the wall. He wants to buy some souvenirs. Yay, I think to myself. Shopping!

The trouble is, we get disoriented and end up in the Muslim section. We try to count turns and get back to the clean Jewish section of the underground shops. We are mixed up in an unfathomable, dark cavernous maze. Neon lights glare from shops, occasional bare bulbs light obscure paths. Steps appear arbitrarily in this creepy network. Malicious, nasty, mean faces greet us, as we get further lost in filthier streets. Our boots tramp through sunflower seeds, melon seeds, and all manner of slop. Garbage is simply strewn in passageways and strange alleys adjacent to shops selling kaffiahs, or burkas, or water pipes, or well ... We just shouldn't be here.

"See those clothes, the Muslims hang them over the security cameras then stab people," Tennessee says. "The IDF can never find out who did it."

"Really?" I say.

"I can get shanked. Look at us. We look like army," Tennessee says to me. A chill runs up my spine at the thought of what would happen to me if Tennessee were to be knifed.

"Okay, let's act like tourists on vacation. Pretend we are shopping for trinkets for our kids back home," I say.

"Quick, turn your jacket inside out. Put the orange side out," Tennessee says. We flip our jackets inside out and manage to zip them up inside out, so no army green is showing. We quickly turn a corner so anyone who saw the switch is gone. We look ridiculous with the bright orange liners as our new "touristy" jackets.

"Oh, look honey! Do you think Junior would like this?" I ask Tennessee pointing to a cross in one of the many Muslim shops. We never stop moving as we desperately try to find our way out of the underground labyrinth. The eighteen-foot-high ancient brick walls line narrow paths and wind in no particular order. The cobblestones underfoot have two parallel grooves worn by hundreds of years of carts. I visualize Roman Centurions pushing or pulling skinny carts full of swords and spears, maybe dead bodies during plague years. The uneven paths provide the perfect place to trip.

We are purposely being loud and stupid sounding as we point to different tchotchkes. If he says he likes something, I hate it, and vice versa. This way we never stop moving long enough to talk, haggle, or get stabbed. My whole thought is to keep Tennessee alive, because if he gets stabbed, the Muslims will have fun and games with me. Quite frankly, I'm allergic to that kind of fun and games.

I notice a poster that says Armenia 1915. "We gotta go this way," I point at the sign, thankful that my husband had worked on a documentary about the Armenian Genocide or I wouldn't know to go this way.

"Why?" Tennessee says.

"It's the Armenian Holocaust! That means the Armenian section is around here somewhere."

"So?"

"Armenians are Christians. Muslims killed millions of them in 1915. Christians don't kill Jews nowadays. Or Bnei Noach's." I smile.

We stop for a beer at a restaurant in the Armenian section, glad to have survived the gauntlet. We turn our jackets around, delighted to see the blue sky again. We follow surface streets back to the Jerusalem square. Along the way, we buy some T-shirts and other souvenirs at Jewish shops. We take pictures in front of one shop that says "Welcome brave tourists," a grim reminder of the current intifada.

Around central Jerusalem, we see some of the guys on the street. Everyone decides to stop at a pizza parlor. We order and pay for our respective slices of pizza. The Italian flag themed restaurant seems happy and modern. The pizza reminds us of home. We describe getting lost in the Wall. Everyone agrees it is tricky. Even if you live here, and speak the language, you can still get lost. On the way out of the restaurant, someone tells me this is the very same pizza parlor that got blown up, about a year ago.

"The Muslim busboy opened the back door and let in the terrorists, so they could blow up some Jews," Ramon says.

"Are you serious? Why do they hire these people?" I say.

"I dunno," Moshe says.

Once back at the Jerusalem square, we meet up with Mike. He tells Tennessee to drive the other vehicle. I ride with Mike on the way back, until he says he is going to hang signs tonight. I think back to the last time I rode with Mike and he was hanging posters. We got in a big argument. I flatly refused to hang any because "I don't know what they say. I don't read Hebrew!" He swore to tell me what they say. I still refused. "For all I know, they could say kill everyone!" The downside was, I was still out until 3:00 A.M., and had to deal with the 6:00 A.M. dog feedings at the kennels. I do not want to be out until 3:00 A.M. again. I decide I will escape to the other vehicle, if they stop for gas.

Sure enough, there is a gas stop. This is my chance. I grab my backpack, and run over to the other vehicle.

Mike yells, "Where are you going?"

I yell back over my shoulder, "I'm going to ride with the Americans."

All the guys in the van are yelling "Stop!" or "No!" I jump into the van, and throw my backpack down. Everyone says there is not enough room for me, but clearly there is.

We drive home. "I don't want to ride with Mike because he is going to stay out all night and the dogs have to be fed in the morning."

Then the awful truth comes out, but it is too late to switch back. "We are going bar hopping and looking for girls," comes a chorus of male voices. So, they have to drag their little sister around as they try to pick up girls.

We drive a little ways, then park, and get out of the van. We walk around. Some of the Yeshiva boys go into different bars. The last remnants of a red-orange streaked sky blend into black. Neon lights flicker. Shops close as taverns open. Across the promenade, a man pulls in a stack of five-gallon buckets with a sign that reads "Four Shekels." They are perfect for bathing the dogs, washing floors, or carrying dog food.

Living in the Shomron, it's imperative if you see something you need, you'd better get it, because there are no stores way out there.

"Don't buy that bucket," Donnie warns.

"It's less than a dollar and I need it for the dogs."

"You can't carry it where we're going."

"I'm buying the bucket." I run over and give the man four shekels just before he pulls the stack inside his metal security gate. I grab a blue bucket thinking at least it is not as bright as the red one I really want.

"They won't let you in anywhere with that."

"Sure they will. Just tell any girl you meet that I'm your retarded sister."

We stop in a bar. I slip my blue bucket under the table. Donnie, Tennessee and I are sitting at a back table drinking beers when Tennessee spots a lone girl at the bar. Tennessee leaves his unfinished beer and returns to the bar to buy another beer. Donnie and I watch from the booth.

"That's not a woman."

"How do you know?" Donnie asks.

"Hands, feet, Adam's apple. Trust me, it's not female."

"You're right. Do you think he knows?

I shake my head.

"Oh my G-d, he doesn't know!"

"This should be interesting." I take a sip of my beer.

We almost pee our pants because Tennessee does not realize this pretty "girl" interested in him; is not a she, but a he. Donnie thinks Tennessee will do what Crocodile Dundee did in the movie. We wait, both holding our breath, thinking at any moment Tennessee is going to feel around in the "woman's" crotch when he figures out that she is a he. Alas, Tennessee doesn't suspect a thing, and keeps flirting with "her." Donnie and I are bored watching Tennessee, so we finish our beers. We feel sorry for him.

We walk up to the bar. Donnie whispers the truth to Tennessee. He does a double take towards the "female," then a second double take. He jumps off his barstool and pushes me in between him and the "girl." My blue bucket squeezes between me and "her." Tennessee's eyes get big, and he instantly puts his arm around me saying something to the effect that I have to save him. We are howling with hysterical laughter. Tennessee is horrified with embarrassment.

The "girl" realizes the jig is up. She looks at the three of us, then at my blue bucket. She flicks her hair back, says, "Humphf," and wiggles away like an old time Hollywood movie star. We watch her dramatic exit to the rear of the bar.

I wink at Tennessee. "Well, she does smell good."

Finally, we head home for real. We tease Tennessee all the way home, or at least until he is laughing at himself.

* * *

Later in the week, one of Avraham's friends, and fellow goat herder, gets arrested for wandering into the Palestinian area with his goats. I don't think he realized it. Goats don't understand borders, and sort of just wander around. The friend gets arrested anyway. Avraham is going to go over and walk the goats back to his friend's house. The trouble is, the baby goats cannot walk that far. The adult goats can walk it, but not the babies. There are about thirty or so babies.

Mike tells me, "We need to go get the goats, and you're not going!"

"Oh yeah, that makes sense. Take all the New York City Jews, who never even visited a farm. But leave the one person from Virginia, who grew up with farms all around, and whose parents even had a farm, at home," I say. "Ummm hum, yup, them subways gots lots of goats in 'em. And, smarty pants, where are you going to put the goats?"

"We'll just put them in the back of the truck," Mike says.

"Oh my G-d, you can't do that!" I say.

"Why not?" Mike asks.

"Because they'll jump out!"

"Why?"

"Because they're goats!" I hold up my hands for emphasis and shake my head "They aren't going to stay where you put them. They are going to be upset when they are separated from their mommies and will try to jump out, to get back to their mommies. They are just goats. It's not natural to be riding in a truck. You have to have something to keep them in the truck.

"Like what?"

"Something to put over them, like chicken wire. You can't just throw them in the back of the truck, and think they are going to sit pretty. Even a dog wouldn't do that."

"Okay, maybe you can go."

Since Mike is building some new kennels he goes over to the building site, and grabs a sheet of four-by-eight-foot rebar. This almost fits perfectly in the back of the pickup. The Ben Boys Shaul and Laeb, Jonathan, Mike and I pile into the truck. We manage to round up the babies, and get them into the bed of the pickup.

Mike isn't sure the rebar will stay in place, and thinks it might be too heavy on the little goats. Laeb is a huge animal lover. So, he gets into the back of the pickup. He lies on his back and holds the rebar off the tiny goats using his hands and feet. All the tiny bodies huddle around Laeb. They snuggle up to the strange two-legged goat. Laeb on his back, in the bed of the truck thoroughly enjoys every second of the two-hour ride back to Tapuach.

Once back in the village, we drive over to Avraham's barn. His two guard Shepherds bark incessantly at us while we unload the tiny goats. By the light of a neon lantern, Laeb passes them to the rest of us, who carry them over to Avraham's barn. We hand off the babies to Avraham. He mixes them in with his flock of goats for the evening. We all go home—Laeb, with a huge smile on his face, and his only topic of conversation for the next three weeks.

Chapter 14
Lessons Learned and Unlearned

Mar 19, 2003 - Zion Boshirian, 51, of Mevo Dotan is shot and killed while driving in his car between Mevo Dotan and Shaked in northern Samaria. The Fatah al-Aqsa Martyrs Brigades claims responsibility for the attack.

Apr 10, 2003 - Staff-Sergeant Yigal Lifshitz, 20, of Rishon Lezion, and Staff-Sergeant Ofer Sharabi, 21, of Givat Shmuel are killed and nine others wounded when Palestinian terrorists opened fire before dawn on their base near Bekaot in the northern Jordan Valley. The PFLP and the al-Aqsa Martyrs Brigades claim responsibility for the attack.

www.jewishvirtuallibrary.org

Back in the kitchen after the morning feeding, I peel off my shredded raincoat, lay the duct tape on the table and make myself a cup of instant coffee.

The Israeli's haven't yet developed their own coffee. Therefore, it is expensive to get ground coffee. Even if you can get the ground coffee, nobody has a coffee pot. Everybody does seem to have those British electric tea kettles. I pour hot water from the tea kettle that used to be in the guy's house, until the previous one in the kitchen burned out. Mike had gone over to the guy's house and took back the tea kettle he had given them to use in their house. Canada is very angry. He had assumed possession of the tea kettle. He runs around the village snarling and whining "Where my tea kettle? Where my tea kettle?" I refill the tea kettle with fresh water to insure that this one doesn't burn up also.

I lay out my clear plastic raincoat on the table, and take a sip of the brown liquid. I rearrange the shreds to where they should be. Okay, it's not really a raincoat, more like a cheap heat-shaped plastic bag with a hood. Barely a rain covering. It cost me two dollars, and really it's only suitable for emergencies. I did not think I would be outside so much in pouring cold rain, so I hadn't brought proper rain gear.

Mike gave the guys what is called a harmonete in Hebrew. They are waterproof and warm army-style jumpsuits. Even the smallest one, was way too big, and the crotch hung down below my knees. The Jerusalem hiking store has raincoats, but they cost eighty-five dollars. I do not feel like spending that much money, so I keep taping this "raincoat" back together, hoping for better weather.

For some puzzling reason, the dogs keep attacking it every time I wear it. "It must sound or smell like something they hate," I think to myself, as I continue the inspection. At least the duct tape is black, but pretty soon this "raincoat" is going to be made entirely out of duct tape. "Hmmm, that might not look too bad," I think. I put my cup down and begin pulling off pieces of black sticky duct tape and work the plastic back together. Tape goes onto plastic and old tape. I try to keep the wrinkles out of my repairs.

Jonathan comes by in sweats ready for his morning jog. "That looks crazy with the tape all over it," he says.

"Well, real raincoats cost eighty-five dollars at the Jerusalem hiking store."

"Oh, forget it, carry on with your tape."

"Why don't you take one of the dogs with you on your run?" I say.

"Nope, don't want to."

"Well, why don't you run around the village instead down to the summit? It will be safer."

"It's boring running around the village. It's a better run to go down the hill."

"If you took a dog, at least you'd have something to defend yourself with."

"Snap pulls whenever I run. Anyway, I hate her," Jonathan says. "She craps in her cage the minute I put her back in it. Then, I have to clean up that shit. I just wanna be alone."

"You could take a different dog for your run; at least you would have some protection with you. Any of the dogs would defend you."

"No way. Then she will get jealous, and crap in her cage even more," he says on his way out the door.

I had tried everything to get Snap to poop outside of her cage to no avail. I even took her on a four-hour walk one morning, when I knew she had to poop. And she still saved it for the cage.

* * *

Years later when I work with a German trainer, he tells me that the German police deliberately train their patrol dogs to only poop in their cages. "They think that it looks weak for a police dog to go to the bathroom in public," he says to me. As soon as he says that, lights go off in my brain about Snap.

* * *

Right now, I do not know these German police dog training concepts. I am at my wits end on how to get Snap to stop pooping in her cage. I never do.

The Ben Boys stop by and get a cup of coffee. Laeb tells me my raincoat is pathetic. Shaul drags hard on his cigarette and says, "whacked." I continue to tape my raincoat back to shape. They put their change on the table and count out their shekels between them. They have just enough money for one pack of cigarettes. Out the door they leave, to hitchhike down to the summit, to the abandoned bus that has been converted into a convenience store.

Daniel Pinner comes by and says, "Mike has arranged for us to use a classroom in Ariel University for our ulpan."

I am really happy about this development because I hate being illiterate, and mute. "That's the best news I've heard. Finally! I get to learn Hebrew."

Pinner looks at my repairs and asks, "Are you making, a clown costume?"

"No, I am fixing my raincoat. The dogs keep attacking it every time I wear it."

Mike drops in and says, "We are going to the army range today." He looks directly at me. "You haven't been your usual complaining self lately.".

"Oh I am, I was just trying the opposite approach."

Since finding Betty, I haven't complained too much about not having a gun. Suddenly, I realize it might be a dead giveaway. In order to make up for my not complaining about my lack of a gun I say, "Well ahh, Whadda ya know. Maybe I'll get a gun after all."

To get to the army range, we go through the Muslim village of Shem, which is what they renamed Jericho. We travel in a pack, fast through the village. Our radios are in communication with each car in our convoy. There are five cars packed with people. We make a wrong turn and quickly turn around. Radios constantly communicate between cars. Finally we make it to the army range.

The shooting range is merely an empty field with a concrete shelter at one end. It is where the trainees shoot. A couple of army men explain the parts and workings of both the M-16 and the Uzi. They show us how to "charge" each gun. That is what they call it "charge the gun." We all start saying "charge the gun," to the point that nobody remembers what the English term is. I know the word is not charge but for the life of me I cannot remember the proper term.

Avraham's seventeen-year-old daughter has trouble charging the Glock. I pull Avraham aside and tell him what Big Tony had told me when I had trouble with his Sig. "In order to charge the gun, you have to act like you are punching the bad guy. Put all your anger and strength into it," I say, repeating Big Tony's lesson.

"Oh, yes, I know," Avraham says dismissively to me.

"No, your daughter is having trouble. She needs to learn this. A man might not be around, and this could save her life, or even the life of your grandkids. You have to tell her," I say to Avraham's flippant comment.

"Yes, yes I know."

"I'm only saying what the cop told me to do because I was having the same problem with the nine millimeter. She needs to learn this. You might not be around," I say.

Avraham finally speaks to her in Hebrew. Her long modest jeans skirt is oddly juxtaposed against the blue steel in her hands. Her long hair hangs braided in a thick twist over one shoulder.

The army trainer hands me an M-16, and says "Try to hit the target out there." I look downrange and at first do not see anything. Then I look closer and realize he is referring to the ammo can on a stick. It blends into the green grass. I am standing, so I charge the gun. I take aim and hit the corner of the can which knocks it off the stick. Since my target is now gone I aim for the stick. Now he wants me to lie down and shoot, so I keep shooting at the stick, chopping it down. He switches me to a different gun, and tells me to stand up, lay down, shoot, shoot.

I give the guns back so another person gets a chance to shoot. The concrete shelter we are in is tagged in Arabic and Hebrew. I have no idea what it says. I wish I could read it. Since it is near an Arab village, most likely it says something derogatory about Israel, or Jews, or the army. One line is crossed out and tagged over in Hebrew. I stare at the writing, hating being illiterate.

Later in the week we go to Ariel University, where we have a class in Hebrew. I am so excited about this, hoping I can learn something. Anything is better than knowing nothing. Daniel Pinner is teaching the class. I am ready with notebook and pen, excited like a child on the first day of school. Not being five-years-old, I just hope my brain isn't too old to learn a new language.

Daniel begins his lesson. It is college level! I am upset and horrified. He continues into the inner meanings of words. I don't even know any words to get to the inner meanings. Pinner continues to break down words into smaller and smaller bits. He talks of kabalistic meanings. I don't even know the ABCs. I get angry.

I raise my hand and ask Pinner, "I am far beneath this level, can you please begin at a lower level?"

Not missing a beat, he continues on in his lecture, which he has obviously carefully prepared. I wish I could understand what he is talking about, but I know nothing. So, I walk out.

Mike walks out too, and wants to know what is wrong.

"This is college level, I am not even kindergarten level, I can't do this. I am too stupid for this class. Everybody else has been to Yeshiva," I say.

"You could try," Mike says to my whines.

"NO, it is so far above me, it is wasting Daniel's time and my time. You know I know no Hebrew. I can't do this." I am on the verge of tears. "I need down and dirty, things like north, south, east, west, up, down, Yossi's been shot, right, left, those kinds of things, not university level inner meanings of words. I need practical stuff, not the poetic definitions. Daniel means well, but he can't teach at such a low level. He's way too smart."

I don't know what became of Daniel's class, but I never went back. I hope Daniel got to teach at the university because he seems like he is good at it, and he likes to teach. You just can't take a kindergartener, and put them in college.

Mike later holds daily classes where he gives some of us vocabulary words. He explains how to say the words and we write them phonetically. This helps somewhat.

* * *

I have guard duty with Moshe again. He has the patience to train some of the dogs and has worked with me a lot to learn tracking. Most of the guys like the drama and to showboat the bite dogs. They get them to bite the sleeve and then they swing them around. It is quite exciting.

Tracking is not anything easily shown off. Usually you are alone, and reading sign, or track, or your dog. It is slow, careful, and methodical. Not everybody likes sprinting behind a dog, or looking for footprints. Moshe is the only one who takes to it.

It is 2:00 A.M. We walk the perimeter. One of the Belgian Malinois is with us. I have a flashlight around my neck on a string. We get the dog to check the fence in places. That's when I notice it, a footprint, rather half a footprint on a rock right near the fence.

"Here, Moshe, take the dog for a minute," I say handing him the leash. He loops the leash over his thumb, even though I have warned all the guys, "Don't do that, because it can break your thumb." He still does it.

I shine the flashlight on the rock. I get down on my knees and look at the muddy toe print sideways. A tennis shoe print is clearly visible on the two foot wide rock. It looks like the perfect place to hop the fence. The print appears to come into the village. The ridges from the imprint of the shoe track are sharp and clear.

"What are you looking at?"

"It's a footprint," I say.

"So? A lot of people walk around here," he says.

"No, I don't think so." I look down the fence line in both directions and back at the rock. "I think somebody hopped the fence right here. Look at this footprint."

"It could have happened anytime in the past day or so," Moshe says.

"No, it couldn't. It started raining hard last night at 7:00 P.M. It finally stopped around midnight. It is now almost 3:00 A.M., so that is what?" I use my fingers and count off the hours. "Eight, nine, ten, eleven, twelve. At least five hours of steady heavy rain. Look at this," I point the flashlight at the rock.

"I don't see anything."

"That's because it is LED light. Things are flat. You have to get sideways to see it." I again squat down and shine the light sideways over the print. "Here, give me the dog. You do it. Get down low and look sideways over the top of the rock." I take the leash and hand him the flashlight. He squats down and inspects the rock like I was doing.

"I see it!"

"So, it has been five hours of continuous rain. The print would have washed away. The edges of the print would be smooth or gone. They are sharp." I say. "If it stopped raining hard around midnight that means this print was put here between midnight and now."

Moshe calls the army. I use orange flagging tape to mark the print for the army. Two men in IDF uniforms come out and inspect the rock. They agree with this assessment. They call a drone, that drops a flare on a tiny parachute. This kind of flare lights up the entire sky as if it is daylight for an about an hour or so. More army men show up. They spread out and search the area. We watch the army in action for a little while.

Then, we continue on the perimeter guard duty because, when the sky is lit in one area, Palestinians often infiltrate at the opposite end of the village. We trudge on through the red clay mud, a light drizzle the only thing left from last night's tsunami.

Later in the week, Mike arranges for a new dog trainer to train the dogs. He allows the villagers to also attend the training sessions if they have a large breed dog.

I previously disagreed loudly with Mike about the Russian dog trainer's methods. His methods do not follow any protocol at all. In fact, he seems to be encouraging poor performances by the dogs.

He reminds me of the old story of the prison that let their prisoners train their man-tracking dogs. The prisoners would get the bloodhounds soaking wet every time they began to track. Finally, when the dogs were sufficiently untrained to man-track, all the prisoners escaped, and the dogs refused to come out to find them.

I watch this supposed "trainer" untrain the dogs. I have already expressed my concern about this guy, yet Mike refuses to listen to me.

We are on the basketball court, and I am working one of the shepherds for the village. For some of the villagers, who come to the training, this is their first time ever training their dogs. They often get too close to one another and some growling occurs. The owners separate to a wider distance. We even lend leashes to some of the villagers who lack them.

We muddle on under the Russian's watchful eye. I still have my doubts about his methods and think they are designed to ruin the dog's previous training. Since I have already said my peace, there is nothing more I can say about it. I just shut up and try to follow along.

Suddenly, without warning or command, the dog I am handling attacks me. He chomps down and begins to shake my hand. I roll on the ground trying to flow with the shakes to avoid losing my entire hand altogether. I go as limp as I can, and try not to pull, resist, or put up any sort of fight. This dog's fun is the fight. Finally, Yossi who is now on crutches due to the gunshot in his ankle, manages to hobble over and get the dog off me.

I stand up and inspect my hand hoping it is not too mauled. It is sliced from the knuckles to beyond the thumb. It is flayed open about two to three inches in width. I can see bone and white stringy cartilage in the middle of a bloody mess of muscle. I remember my pepper spray that I carry on my belt and pull it out of its holster with my left hand. I line it up, and using my left hand thumb and right forearm I press the trigger and squirt the now quietly sitting K-9's face. I empty the canister. The dog doesn't react. "Aaaauuuuugggghhhh!" I scream, then throw the empty canister at the ground.

Turning my back to the dog, I begin an assessment of my hand. I try to move each finger toward my thumb starting with the forefinger, ending with the little finger. The fingers no longer will touch the thumb, and only twitch slightly. They do not move. It looks terrible but isn't painful. "I gotta go to the hospital, I can't feel my hand!" I say.

Moshe has a bandage and he wants to put it on my hand. "This is going to hurt a bit but I am putting it on real tight," he says.

"No! Don't do that," I say pulling my hand away. "You have to shoot that dog now!" I yell at Mike. Mike does not respond.

"We need to put a bandage on," Moshe calmly insists.

Mike seems stunned, it happened so fast.

"Take his gun." I point to one of the guys with a Glock, "and shoot it. If you won't, I will. Gimme the gun, I'll shoot it." My mouth rambles what my hand cannot do.

"We have to stop the bleeding," Moshe says.

"Tie it loose on my hand, the hand has a million little bones and you can break them or you might push the ligaments or other things apart. Things are probably only hanging by a thread. I don't wanna do any more damage."

"But we have to stop the bleeding."

"You can press right here. Under the arm is a major artery, that will stop it." I show him the pressure point under my bicep. He applies pressure, squeezing my arm.

Mike asks "What is the training lesson of spraying the dog with mace after he attacks? Is it a technique?" He really is curious and sincere in wanting to learn the best training methods.

"Nothing, absolutely nothing. It just made me feel good," I say. "If my hand is going to be destroyed, the least that will happen is that dog is gonna get mace in the face. And I'm gonna kill it."

Someone gets a car and Moshe and I get in it. We head for the emergency room. Moshe is going to stay with me to translate. No time to go home, get money, passport, or anything. We zoom out. On the way out, I yell at Mike out the side window of the car, "You better kill that dog!"

Chapter 15
Becoming a Mitzvah

Apr 15, 2003 - Lieutenant Daniel Mandel, 24, of Alon Shvut is killed and another soldier is wounded in an exchange of gunfire during a search for wanted Hamas terrorists in Nablus.

Apr 15, 2003 - Zachar Rahamin Hanukayev, 39, of Sderot and Ahmed Salah Kara, 20, of Shuafat in northern Jerusalem are killed and four Israelis are wounded when a Palestinian terrorist opens fire at the Karni industrial zone crossing in the Gaza Strip. The gunman is killed by security personnel. Hamas claims responsibility for the attack.

www.jewishvirtuallibrary.org

In a large waiting room, Moshe waits with me to see one of two triage admitting doctors.

One wears a yarmulke and one does not. All manner of humanity is waiting for admission to the hospital in Petah Tikvah. There are pregnant women from both sides of the green line, bellies hang low with Jewish and Arab cousins about to make their debut. Stomach aches, broken bones, cuts, scrapes, black eyes, tumors and me with a dog bite, wait for our number, our turn to see one of the doctors. Secretly, I wish to see the one with the yarmulke.

My number is called. Moshe and I make our way to the front of the room to see one of the doctors. "Dang, I really wanted to see the one wearing the kippah," I say to Moshe. He is silent. He explains to the doctor what is wrong with my hand. The doctor speaks no English.

"No problem, we will have you sewn up in no time and you can be on your way," Moshe translates what the doctor says.

"What!" I say. I pull my hand away from the doctor. My eyes squint at him.

"He says it is not a problem and they can stitch you up right away," Moshe translates further.

"No way! You are not going to stitch me up!" I say.

I look at the doctor and ask him, "Are you Jewish?" He doesn't answer me.

Moshe scolds me. "You can't ask that! We don't discriminate in this country according to religion."

"I can too ask. It's my hand, and I will do what I want. I don't care what the law is. Tell them to call the army and arrest me. I don't care. It's my hand. If he is a Christian, he would be proud of it and would say, 'No I am Christian.' If he is Russian atheist, he would say, 'I don't believe in G-d.' The fact that he refuses to answer proves he is a Muslim and wants to hide it." I point to the harried doctor wearing a kippah. "I want to see that guy."

"You can't. He's busy," Moshe says to me. "They are both qualified. You have to take who they give you. You have to go in order."

"I'll wait."

"It could take all night, everyone else gets to go before you," Moshe warns me.

"Fine, I don't care, I'll wait all night if I have to."

"You have to take the doctor they give you. It is against the law to discriminate," Moshe says.

"Look, I am no doctor, but even I know you can't just sew up a wound like this. How does he know that I don't have a broken bone or torn cartilage, ligaments or nerves? The least that has to happen is an X-ray. You can't just sew it up, it can get infected underneath. Then I will lose the use of my right hand." I take a breath. "Or maybe that is what this guy wants."

"They are both good doctors. It will take all night," Moshe says.

"I'll wait, and if this Jew can't see me, I'll wait until the next shift for another Jew. That guy just wants to sew it up. I think he wants me to lose the use of my right hand. You can leave, I'll figure it out. If they want to arrest me for being prejudiced, fine! Even if they take me to prison, I am not letting that guy work on my hand!"

Hours later, after the room clears of almost everyone, the doctor wearing a kippah sees me. He takes one look at my hand, and says I have to go upstairs to the hospital. I do not expect that. My eyes open wide with astonishment. I think an X-ray and some tests are in order, something like that, but I do not expect to be put in the hospital. Moshe calls someone for a ride home.

My hand is bandaged and I am shown to a hospital room. Nobody speaks English. Finally, a nurse who speaks broken English tells me, "Right now, this your room. Soon, we put a woman in the bed." She points to the other bed in the room. I had missed the hospital dinner, but they manage to find me a tray of food to eat. I do not realize I am so hungry, and scarf down the food.

I look at the empty bed and remember all the pregnant Palestinian women in the emergency room. There is no way I want to share a room with a woman giving birth to a future terrorist. Perusing my pile of clothes, folded neatly on the chair beside the bed, I remember the shirt I was wearing says "Dog Trainer" in Hebrew, Russian and English on the back. Muslims have more of an aversion to dogs than they do to pigs. So, I pick up my "Dog Trainer" T-shirt. I find a way to lay the T-shirt casually over the back of the chair so the "Dog Trainer" writing is prominently displayed. I angle the chair so anyone entering the room will see "Dog Trainer" right away. Hopefully, if the hospital tries to put a pregnant terrorist breeder in the next bed, she will see "Dog Trainer" then freak out, run away, and refuse to room with me; but not in any prejudiced way.

Mike has given me a Mers telephone, but it has no minutes. I can receive calls but cannot dial out. Anyway my husband does not have that phone number. I had planned on going into Ariel to buy some minutes, but got bit. My personal phone is not charged up. I look at both useless phones.

I turn on my cell phone hoping it has a tiny amount of charge. I call my husband in America. It goes through. The answering machine picks up. Speaking like a southern auctioneer I say, "I got bit by a dog, I'm fine, I'm in the hos—" The line goes dead. I turn the phone off.

The normal time I talk with my husband is 10:00 A.M. Israeli time. If I keep the phone off except for ten minutes from 10:00 A.M. to 10:10 A.M. Maybe he will call at exactly that time.

Maybe the phone will recharge just enough to receive a phone call. Daily, I turn the phone on for those precious ten minutes hoping my husband will call at precisely that moment.

The next morning begins what becomes a daily ritual for the next three weeks. A doctor followed by a group of six to eight interns comes into my room. Nobody speaks English. Due to Mike's language classes I have learned the word for dog is kelev. So every day, a group of people comes into my room, and the lead doctor says, "blah blah blah kelev blah blah hock-a-loogie, kelev blah blah blah." Then he puts on gloves and inspects my hand.

Some days, the lead doctor is a Muslim. How do I know the doctor is a Muslim, if many of the Jewish doctors do not wear yarmulkes, you might ask? When the lead doctor triple gloves his hands, before inspecting my kelev-bite-hand, I think that is a dead giveaway.

One day, when Dr. Triple Glove is inspecting my hand, I spook him by saying "awhhhh" and shaking my hand quickly towards his face. He no longer comes back very often.

Israeli hospital food is gourmet compared to American hospital food. Breakfast is a dairy meal with many soft cheeses, yogurt, fruits, juice, tea or instant coffee. Lunch is smallish and dinner is a meat meal.

There is no TV in the hospital, unless you pay 300 shekels a day, so there is not much to do. Magazines are useless to me, still being illiterate and all. Fortunately, they are building some offices or apartments right outside my window. That becomes my entertainment. I watch the cranes and construction workers do their thing. It isn't the greatest entertainment I suppose, but it is better than looking at a brick wall.

During the day I am required to soak my hand for hours and hours in Polydine solution, except on the days when I am scheduled for an operation. I end up having three operations total to restore the use of my hand. Most of the time I am bored to tears, and most grateful for any visitor. I even look forward to the Bedouin woman who comes in daily to mop or, should I say, squeegee my floor. We cannot communicate. We simply smile at each other. Me, cross legged on the bed with my right hand in a bowl of black iodine and her on the floor wiping up black muddy water is somehow oddly profound.

Every day except Shabbat, Mike or some of the guys come for a visit. "Emmanuel is back, and his gun is missing." Mike tells me. I look at him and try not to look surprised.

"Do you know anything about Emmanuel's gun?" Mike persists.

"Did you kill that dog?" I ask.

"Emmanuel is running around the village with a big ol' buck knife," Shaul says.

"Yeah, he carries a sharpening stone, and sharpens his knife and says, "Where my gun?" Laeb says.

"He sounds exactly like the Terminator," Shaul says.

"He does like this with the knife." Laeb demonstrates how Emmanuel sharpens his knife. "And all he says is 'Where my gun? Where my gun?'"

"Wow," I say.

"How do you walk your dog?" Mike asks.

"On a leash," I say with a puzzled expression on my face.

"Even Laeb can't walk your dog," Shaul says.

"Really?"

Shaul, Laeb's brother shows how Laeb looks trying to walk my small hound. All six feet four, two hundred pounds of Shaul stands and demonstrates being severely pulled every which way by my dog, who is only slightly bigger than a Beagle. Everyone busts up laughing at Shaul's imitation of Laeb being dragged all over the village by Po-poki.

"Ooooh, are you using the red collar that's on him?" I ask.

"Yes," Laeb says.

"Of course you can't walk him; you have to use the spiked collar. It's on the back of the door knob. He'll pull you all over the place, if you use the soft collar," I say.

"Man, that dog is strong. I thought I was doing something wrong," Laeb says.

"Naw, he's a man-tracker. He never was trained to heel. That's why you have to use the spikes," I say.

I even appreciate Pinner's jokes, and laugh heartily with him, when he visits. I explain to everyone why the "Dog Trainer" shirt is hanging on the chair. We laugh about Dr. Triple Glove.

Mike brings me the English-Hebrew Torah, to read. I ask him to bring me the charger to my phone. He brings the wrong charger, then my computer charger, or some other charger, then he brings the electric converter, my computer. He never finds my phone charger. Nobody visiting has any minutes on their phones, so I cannot borrow theirs.

Every time I go for an operation, they tell me I will get to go home afterward. After the first operation I am happy to leave the hospital. But they renege, and tell me my hand is more messed up than they thought, and I have to stay. By the second operation, when they again say I have to stay, I begin to feel like a prisoner. I plan a hunger strike.

With the language barrier, I have to plan my protest sign words carefully. "Hell no, we won't go," won't work. "Hell no, I won't go to operation," is no good, because I still cannot hold a pencil, so I need another operation. "Fix my hand, I want to go home" implies they are bad doctors. I ask one nurse to write "hunger" on a paper and another nurse how to write "strike." I figure my sign will at least need to say "hunger strike" but I haven't figured out the exact words yet.

Then, I remember a documentary about the Suffragettes who protested to get the women's vote in America. They were jailed. When the ladies went on a hunger strike, the men ran tubes down their throats and force fed them. This isn't America. I tear up the two pieces of paper. My plans for a brilliant hunger strike quashed by the very real possibility of a tube shoved down my throat.

* * *

Back in America, my husband after a week, hasn't heard from me. He begins to worry and calls my mother in Virginia. He tells my mom that I am in Israel somewhere in the West Bank. He doesn't know what happened to me, and he hasn't heard from me. My mom calls my husband daily asking about me. I am still trying for those ten minutes a day to receive a phone call. I try with all my might to send the ESP to my husband to call at 10:00 A.M. We are going on the second Shabbat with no communication.

My husband talks with Segi, an Israeli actor and friend who has worked on some movies with us. He was a Golani Commander before coming to America to pursue his movie star dream. He is fluent in Hebrew, but has never heard of Apple Village which is the literal translation of K'far Tapuach. He is willing, however, to go and find this place and me. Friday afternoon, John talks with Segi and tells him that Sunday he will buy two tickets to Israel for a rescue mission if he doesn't hear from me. Plans are finalized for this international Search and Rescue mission. He calls my mom and tells her the plan. At this point he doesn't know I am bit, or in the hospital, or anything.

* * *

There is a mitzvah lady who is in the hallways of the hospital with a cart full of things people might need. She has feminine hygiene products, since the hospital does not provide them. She has many other things too. On Shabbat, she brings candles on her cart for any of the Jewish ladies to light. Open flames are not allowed in the rooms. I go out into the hallway and light candles, then thank her.

Sunday, my husband tries at 10:00 A.M. Israeli time to call and it comes through. "Oh thank G-d, shut up and listen. My phone doesn't have a charge. I got bit by a dog. I am in the hospital. I am okay. It is only my hand. I am okay. They did an operation. I am okay," I say. We talk a little bit more then the phone goes dead. Later he tells me about the rescue mission, canceled much to the dismay of our good friend Segi.

* * *

The time spent in hand soaks is only broken up by the operations where I am knocked out, fully unconscious. I thoroughly enjoy any visitor. I spend the rest of my time reading Torah or watching construction.

During the last week, one particularly lonely night, Mike comes in for a visit. He is followed by many of the dog handlers, and the Ben Boys. Shaul is wearing sunglasses even though it is nighttime. Everyone is giggling, and trying not to laugh out loud.

"What's going on?" I ask. They all stifle laughter.

Smiling, I ask, "Come on guys, what's going on?"

They keep giggling.

Then, I notice Shaul has my dog on a leash. His orange Search and Rescue vest is inside out. My dog sees me, and immediately jumps up onto the bed where I am sitting.

"Get him off the bed! He cannot be on the bed!" Mike says.

"Why? He always jumps on the bed," I say.

"Because he is a blind dog."

I start laughing, and finally understand why Shaul has on sunglasses at 9:00 P.M. I get Po-poki off the bed and Shaul demonstrates his blind act. Everyone laughs and giggles and we have a great visit.

"We found something under your bed," Mike says.

"Oh you mean the brick?" I say

"Is that what you call it?"

"No, actually her name is Betty."

Laeb offers, "We were trying to take your dog out for a walk, and he was hiding under the bed, and we found Emmanuel's..."

"Brick. You found Emmanuel's brick," I say, cutting him off, remembering that seven-year prison thing for unauthorized weapons. "And my dog doesn't hide for anyone. You guys were looking. Since you're snooping all over my house, you can bring me some underwear," I say, knowing full well how immodest that is. They would later make Ari get the underwear because he has twelve sisters.

Finally, it is time for them to go home. Shaul puts his sunglasses on, and gets his seeing eye dog act back together. They all leave. I sleep with a huge grin this time. I think most of the guys on this mission did too.

Later in the week, I finally get to meet the surgeon who operated those three times on my hand. He did everything possible to restore the use of it. He worries he did not do enough because I have nerve damage on two of my fingers that he could not repair. "I am sending you to plastic surgery, they will finish your hand," he says.

"That's Okay, I don't want any more operations."

"But you will have a very bad scar."

"It's Okay. Really I don't need my hand to be pretty. I'm happy. See?" I pick up a pen from his desk. "I can pick up a pen. That's all I care about. See?" I give him a picture of me with one of the dogs. Then I sign it for him. "To the best surgeon in Israel, Thank you, XXOO, Devorah." To me this seems perfectly natural, having worked in Hollywood most my life, but he looks slightly puzzled at the photograph.

"Then, I am releasing you. Be sure to come back next week for rehabilitation."

I look at my hand with the ugly black stitches over a shocking red line tinged with yellowish iodine stains. "Do I have to?"

"Yes." He shows me the difference between the left and right hands. "I had to use the skin from the web to close the hole. It will tighten up if you do not do the exercises."

Chapter 16
Miracles

Apr 20, 2003 - IDF photographer Corporal Lior Ziv, 19, of Holon, is killed and three other soldiers are wounded during an operation to destroy a Hamas smuggling tunnel in Rafah, in the Gaza Strip.

Apr 24, 2003 - Alexander Kostyuk, a 23-year-old security guard from Bat Yam, is killed and 13 are wounded, two seriously, in a suicide bombing outside the train station in K'far Sava. Groups related to the Fatah al-Aqsa Martyrs Brigades and the PFLP claim joint responsibility for the attack.

www.jewishvirtuallibrary.org

It is a warm and beautiful spring day with clear blue skies and bougainvillea blooming in front of the hospital. Elihav picks me up from the hospital in his black Nissan. I hand him a spinach and cheese boreacha. Right before leaving, I had bought a bag of them in the basement of the hospital. Elihav lustily grabs the crumbly pastry and takes a couple of bites. We take off out of the circle in front of the clean modern white stone faced building.

Speeding down the street, all of a sudden, he screams "aughhh" and throws the pastry out the window. He brakes for a red light.

"What's wrong?" I look around. I think perhaps he spies a terrorist or something I am not aware of. I see nothing. Nobody has cut him off in traffic. I cannot figure out his bizarre behavior.

"The pastry!" he screams.

"It's only spinach and cheese, are you allergic to spinach?" I'm completely baffled by his weird behavior. "Or cheese?" We enter the freeway.

"I spent all Sunday cleaning my car," he screams over the roar of the engine and the sound of the wind blowing through the windows.

"So, I don't get it. What's the big deal?"

"I cleaned it for Pesach, I spent all day vacuuming, now my car is a mess. I will have to clean it all over again," he says to me.

"Isn't Passover a week away?" I ask.

"Yes, but I like to get a jump on things."

I close the bag containing three more of the crumbly pastries and push it out of his sight. We ride back to Tapuach in silence.

Back in the village, I unload my things and reacquaint myself with my dog and the village's dogs. Everyone in the village wants to see my hand and says they were praying for me, but when they see the bright red scar and black stitches they get a bit grossed out.

Mostly I ignore the looks of my hand, and constantly give thanks for opposable thumb usage. I relentlessly pick at the itchy scar between re-hab appointments, until I am able to remove the stitches. I stop going to rehab after two weeks, and just do the exercises at home.

I go to the kitchen and ask Mike where the dog is that bit me. Mike looks up from his newspapers and gives me some silly non-answer. I let him know in no uncertain terms that I intend to kill the dog before I leave Israel and how I consider it a mitzvah to do so. Mike says something to Moshe in Hebrew. Moshe quickly leaves.

My eyes follow Moshe as he hurriedly exits the kitchen. "What? Oh, I get it. You have him in the witness protection program." I say.

"Oh no, I was only telling Moshe to make up the schedule for next week," Mike says.

"Oh yeah, sure. We haven't had a schedule since forever. I'm gonna find that dog and when I do, he dies."

"What are you gonna kill him with? You don't have a gun anymore," Mike says, practically taunting me.

"I dunno, but he dies."

"I've been analyzing why he bit you, and I think . . ."

"I don't give a damn why he bit me. I'm the handler, you're just lucky he bit me and not some kid in the village. What if he bit a kid? It would destroy a kid's life!

"Has v'Shalom."

You can't hide him forever, I'm gonna find him and kill him!" I level my eyes to Mike's. "I'll be back this evening, I need to get something in Ariel." I leave the kitchen.

In Ariel, I get off the bus before entering the security gates. I cross the street past the Muslim lady who sells fresh vegetables, and hike up the incline from the gas station to the Ariel hotel. Entering the lobby, I walk the wrought iron decorated staircase down to the gun range. Since I cannot buy a gun, I buy the biggest knife they have. "I'll have to tie the dog up before I stab him or slice him open. This could get gross," I think. "Antifreeze!" What is the word for antifreeze? I mumble to myself.

I leave the gun range and cross over to the gas station. I ask the attendant for antifreeze. He doesn't know what that is because he has only a cursory command of English. I hadn't brought my dictionary so I do not know the Hebrew word. I vow to come back and buy some antifreeze unless I can find the dog and kill it with my new knife first. Antifreeze is the back up and could be cruel. I figure I will just stick with the knife. "I hope I don't faint when I do this," I think.

* * *

Back in Tapuach, Mike comes over to my house and gives me a white fluffy dog. He says it is only four months old but it is already about seventy pounds and stands four inches taller on the back than my dog. The dog's white fur is matted and stained red from playing or being kept in the mud.

"That thing is gonna be huge when it gets full grown," I say.

"That's why the father got it for his daughter," Mike says. "She's getting married in a couple of weeks. Her and her fiancé intend on moving to a hilltop and living there, like "Hilltop Youth." They will be all alone on the hill surrounded by Arabs," Mike says.

"Wow."

"Can you teach it to guard?" Mike asks.

"Not in three weeks, I can't." The dog lays down.

"Can you try?"

I bend over and check the dog's teeth. "That's a puppy! It doesn't even have permanent teeth. I can't teach it much. Maybe I can get it to sit. You really shouldn't start bite work without permanent teeth."

"Well, she's moving to a hilltop in three weeks, and her father is worried."

"I'll do what I can, but it is not a fully-trained dog. She shouldn't rely on such a young dog for total protection.

"Do what you can. I am sure you can do something."

"I'll try to get it house broken. You better not tell them it's a fully trained dog, either. Maybe she should borrow one of our dogs for a little while."

"She hates our dogs."

"She shouldn't rely on a puppy. It's going to be a huge dog, but right now it is only a puppy. It might not look like a puppy, but it's still puppy-brained."

"I promised her dad."

"Maybe you could convince her to take one of our dogs, just for a couple of months."

"She doesn't like our dogs. She says they are too aggressive."

The next day, I walk my dog with the new puppy which I call Fluffy for obvious reasons. Fluffy pees in my house numerous times, but finally catches on to the bathroom being outside. Fluffy doesn't like going for walks and seems very lazy, but at night she stays up and roams around in circles. When I do finally check on the breed, I learn this particular breed sleeps during the day but stays up and guards livestock all night. "That would explain the nightly wanderings," I think as I log off the Internet.

Using an old sock with a knot tied in the middle, I play tug-o-war with Fluffy, the beginning basics of bite work. Finally I get Fluffy to hold and tug on the sock. There's not much more I can do because she only has baby teeth, and I don't pull too hard. Fluffy learns "sit" pretty quickly, but I still practice every day at least twice a day. Po-poki also plays tug-o-war with Fluffy.

* * *

My husband is coming for a couple of week's visit. Mike tells the Ben Boys to drive me to the airport and pick him up. At the airport, Shaul and Laeb start picking out different men coming through arrivals as to who might be my husband. Laeb wants to know why I do not have a photo in my wallet of John. I have no idea why I do not carry a picture of him.

"I think carrying a picture is a man thing. Most women carry pictures of their children, not their husbands," I say watching the line. I wonder if I am weird for not having a picture of John in my wallet.

They keep picking out anyone with an aloha shirt.

"My husband is Hawaiian. I have no idea if he is wearing a Hawaiian shirt. He's Hawaiian. We are looking for a Hawaiian person, not a Hawaiian shirt."

"Well, what does a Hawaiian look like?" Laeb asks.

"I don't know, like brown skin, black hair." I try to think of a distinguishing characteristic of Native Hawaiians. "They look kind of Sephardic."

Finally, my husband walks through. We hug. The Ben Boys agree Hawaiians look Sephardi. In fact, once John learns a few phrases in Hebrew, most people think he is Sephardic.

With my husband in town, Mike has to step up his K-9 witness protection program. He keeps moving the dog that bit me from house to house so I cannot find it. He is not at this point convinced the dog needs to die. The dog cost at least ten to twenty thousand to buy. If you add the additional trainings, food, equipment, and housing, it could be closer to thirty-five to fifty thousand all told. To kill it seems very unreasonable and wasteful.

In the kitchen at breakfast, Mike tells everyone there has been a shooting out on a remote farm. We need to go there. He wants me to bring my dog, to possibly track. We pack two vehicles with many young men and head out to the sheep farm. It is isolated; wild, and beautiful, with tall steep cliffs all around. We have ten or more young men with us.

On the way in, we see a new car that has been in the weirdest wreck imaginable. I leave Po-poki in the truck in his crate. The car? Last week the car hit a landmine on the very same road, we have only a few minutes ago arrived by.

"When the son came home, he ran over the bomb. It blew him out of his car like Donald Duck," Mike translates.

Moshe uses his thumb to show how the guy blew up and out of his car. "He landed in the field. He wasn't hurt. Maybe a scratch or two, that is all." We all stare in disbelief. Someone says miracle.

Everyone says, "Baruach HaShem."

Last night, they had no guard on duty in the tower. With no guard, the terrorists attacked. They shot at the two houses.

"Hmmm, seems like somebody had inside information about the guard," I say to no one in particular.

We walk around with the younger of the men who lives here. There are two houses. The father and his wife live in one, and the son and his wife live in the other. Last night, a couple of Palestinians snuck up to the house. They placed themselves in such a way that one was on one side of the house, and the other on the other side of the house. They were both shooting at the house trying to kill any Jews inside. It was truly a stupid plan on their part, because if they miss the Jews, they were in essence shooting at each other. The house with the Jews inside was in the crossfire.

We look at both sides of the house at all the holes from the AK-47s of both terrorists. The holes look to be about waist high to anyone inside. With all those hundreds of rounds shot, not one Jew inside was hit. They had been shooting at the father's house. The son who lives next door, heard the shooting and grabbed his Uzi, came outside, and shot at the terrorists. He killed one immediately. Then, one of the shots he fired hit the other terrorist's gun in such a way that it bent the slot where you stick the magazine. The terrorist could not reload. They were then able to kill that terrorist.

It wasn't until daylight when the army could get out there. The terrorists lay on the ground dead until sun up. Their blood had seeped into the dirt. It is now about high noon, and you can still see the spots of blood on the dirt between the houses.

Elihav tells me to go and get my dog, to find out where they came from.

I try to tell him "my dog doesn't do that."

"Why not? He's a sniffer dog isn't he? I can smell the terrorist blood; surely your dog can smell it. Can't you smell it?" Elihav says.

"Yes, I can smell cadaver; but being able to smell something doesn't mean he can track in the wrong direction. My dog goes forward. This is the end of the line. My dog doesn't go backwards. What you want is a backtracker."

"Well, go get your dog then."

"If you want a dog to go backwards, you have to train a dog specifically for that. Dogs can only go one direction, not both," I say.

"But I can smell it," Elihav says, indicating the putrid odor emanating from the bloodstained dirt.

"Look, this is the end of the trail. If I scent my dog where is he going to go? This is where the guy died. He did not move from here. Unless you want me to track the dead body to the army base? And, why would I do that? Where do you want me to go?"

"Find out where he came from, what village," Elihav says.

"He is not trained for that. This is the end of the line. There is no more terrorist to track. He's dead! You need a different dog if you want to go that way," I say. Elihav doesn't get it.

Remembering Sonja, the FBI agent I used to train with, who went to the Twin Towers on 9/11, she said, "People on the rubble pile would get a whiff of a dead body and yell 'HERE, HERE, WE NEED A CADAVER DOG OVER HERE.'" She kept telling people "If you can smell it, you do not need a dog. The dog is for when you can't smell it." I am making about the same headway with Elihav. He does not understand the dog's purpose or abilities.

Mike interrupts and asks everyone to go up the hill and pray the prayer for when someone narrowly escapes death. I do not know the prayer, but know of it. We all trek up the hill to the stone synagogue this family hand-built on the highest point. Inside it is so beautiful with hand-carved wood walls and benches. A master carpenter must have built the little temple. Study books line the walls. Light streams through the windows, illuminating the precious building like magical stained glass.

Mike knew this courageous hilltop family would need to pray, so he made sure to bring enough men to make a minyan. Ever since Avraham prayed to G-d to save Sodom & Gomorrah for the sake of one hundred, then fifty, then forty, thirty, finally he stopped at ten righteous men; Jewish men always pray with at least ten men. That way, they can be sure G-d is listening. However, it only takes one woman to pray, but ten men have to join forces to be heard by G-d.

"I'll just hold up the women's section," I say to the guys. It is one of those strange Orthodox rules that, well, what can they say? That G-d thinks women are inferior like they sometimes think? Or, admit G-d listens to women, perhaps even more than men, since He only requires one of us.

Being the only female, I am shown to the "women's section." It is a bench in the corner with a curtain you can pull all around yourself. The women's section is smaller than a teensy-tiny RV shower. I am not claustrophobic, but this feels like being in a box.

"Forget it, I'm going outside and talk to G-d," I say. I head outside for the breathtaking vistas and lush slanted fields atop this mountain. The sheep bleat from the steel barn off to the right. With the first spring flowers starting to come up, why would I want to stay in a box when I can view G-d's handiwork up close?

Moshe stands in the doorway of the synagogue watching me, M-16 ever at his side. He prays with the men, yet keeps a watchful eye on the woman in the field.

Chapter 17
Enough

> Apr 30, 2003 - Ran Baron, 23, of Tel Aviv, Dominique Caroline Hass, 29, of Tel Aviv, and Yanai Weiss, 46, of Holon, are murdered and about 60 people are wounded when a suicide bomber blows himself up at a beachfront pub, "Mike's Place," in Tel Aviv. The Fatah Tanzim and Hamas claim responsibility for the attack, carried out as a joint operation.
>
> *www.jewishvirtuallibrary.org*

My husband, John makes a phone call to Karen. She used to be one of his students at Columbia College, Hollywood. She gives him her address and wants us to come over so she can "show us around." We let Mike know we will be gone for the day and quickly get ourselves down to the bus stop at the summit (the bottom of the hill). We find our way to Tel Aviv and since we do not know the busses very well, we hop a cab.

The taxi driver lets us out in an exclusive neighborhood in front of one building. We have to use a phone to call Karen so she can buzz us into the building. We don't notice the cab driver is also waiting. As soon as Karen appears, the taxi driver goes into a rant with her in Hebrew. In typical Israeli fashion, she yells back. Then, she hands him a twenty shekel note.

"We paid him already," I say.

"He says you didn't pay," Karen says.

"We did pay him," John says.

"That's okay its nothing," Karen says. The taxi driver leaves.

"Sounds like a scam to me," I say.

"It's okay, it is only a tip. Come on." She waves for us to follow her.

We head into her building and take the elevator up to her mom's apartment. I am amazed by the decorating and beauty of the apartment. I am especially impressed with her furniture. It all matches, and is not broken.

"Where are you staying at?" Karen questions my sanity for living in a place "like that." She has never heard of K'far Tapuach and most assuredly has never been to the West Bank. "Most Israelis do not go there."

Karen wants to take us to the beach. She especially wants to take us to some beachfront restaurant that serves "toast." She drives her car. I sit in the backseat as she and my husband discuss old college days. I wonder what is this "toast" she keeps talking about. We park on the main street. It runs parallel to the beach. We walk a couple of blocks and cross over to this famous beachfront restaurant for "toast."

She rents a yellow-striped cabana. We drag over some beach chairs and settle in for a fun day at the beach. Karen is wearing sling backs, and slips them off. John takes off his boots and socks. I take off my new boots that have just arrived from the Magnum Boot Company last week with a letter apologizing for their boots splitting apart at the seams. We wiggle our toes in the white Israeli sand.

We watch the skinny Muslim bodybuilders pretend they are at Muscle Beach in Venice, California. Karen orders "toast." I am still wondering what is this "toast." My mouth waters at the thought of a new Israeli delicacy.

The waiter brings us some beers and says the "toast" will be ready in a bit as they are shorthanded. Clinking beer bottles, we toast to good friends, and college and movies and Hollywood and anything else we can think of. Rolling up our pants, we laugh and giggle and run into the surf. We run up to the cabana exactly in time to meet the waiter who has brought our "toast."

"But this is just toast." I pick up a piece of toasted sourdough bread with some pesto and cheese.

"Yes, isn't it wonderful," Karen says.

"Oh yeah, it's great!" John says. He greedily plops his toast into his mouth.

I wonder as I eat the toast, if they even sell toasters in Israel. I vow to check the next time I am near an appliance store.

We leave the beach stuffed with beer and "toast." We begin the journey back to the car. It didn't seem as far when we arrived, but the walk back seems to go on forever. Karen cannot find the car. She swears she parked it right here, but it's gone. In fact there are no cars on the road at all.

"No, it is perfectly fine to park here." She points to the street sign. She re-reads it. I stare at the sign and Hebrew lettering.

"Are you sure?" I ask.

"Yes, this is perfectly okay to park here. There is no warning," Karen says. Then, she asks at a shop what happened to all the cars that were parked on the street. The shop owner says they all got towed, but he doesn't know where. We follow Karen like puppies. She heads back to the beachfront restaurant.

"That's the American embassy right there. You could go there if you want," she says to us.

"No way," I say. "The last time I went to the American embassy was in Kenya. The very next day it got blown up. I think it is better for the Marines if I do not go to the embassy."

"Well, there it is, right over Mike's Place," she says pointing to one of the buildings in the near distance.

"What's that?" John asks.

"It's a bar and nightclub."

"I think jazz bands play there. It's world famous," I say.

Karen stops a policewoman and asks in Hebrew where they tow cars. She is told where the impound lot is, and that is the direction we begin walking.

We slog on forever. I am bored and my feet hurt. So, I make up a movie I think the two of them should make. "This Secular guy gets lost or broken down in the desert of Israel and . . . what is his motive for being there? Uhhh. A Secular guy has to go to a funeral for his mother out in the outback of Israel, and he breaks down in his car. Along the way he meets many weird people who offer to help or who join his quest until there are hundreds of people following him around: a Rasta Orthodox pot smoking guy, a black hat dude, a Bedouin camel driver, and a . . ."

"Shut up, we're here," Karen says cutting off forever my Academy Award winning movie. We turn and walk into the car impound lot.

She finds her car and begins to yell at the Muslim owners. John acts like big brother and keeps his mouth shut so they don't know he doesn't understand a word of her conversation. I look around at the many men in the yard and think they are up to something. Karen says she was parked legally, and they had no right to tow her car.

There seems to be a lot of shuffling with all the Muslim males hanging around. When you travel in countries where you don't know the language, you rely on your sixth sense. In fact, that sense always seems to intensify under these circumstances. I've always believed it was the body's protection mode. "Something doesn't look right. They look guilty of something," I say.

John takes out his video camera and starts filming. A bunch of the guys start yelling at him. They circle threateningly around him. They make it quite clear they do not want him filming.

"For sure they are up to something. I don't know what it is, but they are definitely up to something," I say. Under my breath to John I say, "No matter what, keep filming, something's up." John keeps filming. Even after he pretends to stop, he keeps the camera rolling.

With all of Karen's yelling, screaming, and arm shaking, she still ends up paying a fee. I think it is about thirty US dollars. We hop in her car and she races to get us to the bus station so we can catch the seven o'clock bus out of Tel Aviv. There are other busses out of Tel

Aviv, but this is the absolute last bus we can take to make the connecting bus in Ariel. If we miss it, we will be stranded in hostile territory—overnight. We make it with literally two minutes to spare. We don't even say "good-bye" and "thank you." We only wave to her out the side window of the bus.

The next morning, at breakfast, the kitchen is abuzz. Mike and everyone is talking about the bombing in Tel Aviv. Last night, Mike's Place, the Jazz Club, had a suicide bomber. The story is not clear. Five, six, eight, a dozen people are dead. Nobody knows for sure. Many people are injured. The explosion happened during a concert.

According to Jewish law, every drop of blood, guts, skin, or flesh of a Jew must be buried. And, it must be buried within 24 hours. When they have these kinds of bombings, the government relies on the civilian Orthodox volunteer group Zaka to pick up all the body parts. Bits of brain matter are often found blocks away in a tree, or on somebody's car windshield, or on a roof, maybe on a baby's highchair left out on a balcony overnight. Tiny blood splatters and droplets are soaked up with clean white cotton balls and placed gently in plastic bags for burial. Care is given to every bit of a Jewish body by these heroic men, who often suffer PTSD themselves, by their very work.

"We were just there," John says.

"What band was playing?" I ask.
"Who cares," Daniel says.
"Well, I wouldn't want to be that band," I say.

My husband and I go to the kennels and take care of the morning feedings and shmira. No matter what happens, the dogs still need to be fed and worked. We continue to train Fluffy and the dogs in the kennels.

We manage to do a little touring before his three weeks are up.

* * *

Mike drives my husband to the airport when it is time for him to leave Israel. The three of us wait in line for John to get his baggage X-rayed. Mike starts talking in Hebrew to the female Israeli soldier who is doing the screening.

"Tell him not to talk for me," John hisses at me.

Before I can say a word to Mike, the beautiful soldier sends my husband over to the Palestinian line. John moves grudgingly over to the other line, and starts angrily yelling. "Now look where I am! I told you not to talk for me! Look at me! I am in the terrorist line! Look at where I am! Look! Look at this!"

I have rarely seen him this angry. For him to yell in public is quite out of character.

"Just leave me alone. Don't talk for me!"

Mike and I walk slightly away from the line and wait for him to be scrutinized. "Looks like your husband is mad at you," Mike says to me.

"Oh no, my husband is not mad at me. He is mad at *you*! And you better hope he gets on the plane or he's gonna kick your ass."

Finally, another soldier indicates for my husband to get back into the Jewish line. He calms down. John is quickly inspected and boards the plane back to Los Angeles.

Mike doesn't even attempt small talk on the ride back to Tapuach.

* * *

Fluffy's new owner is now married. It has been a couple of weeks and she still hasn't picked up her puppy dog. Finally, I get a call from the bride. A station wagon pulls up in front of my house and Israel's latest Mr. and Mrs. get out of the white car.

I have given her puppy a bath in my own bathtub, much to the horror of her new husband. He looks at me like I am a disgusting, insane, filthy person for bathing the dog in my bathtub. Even when I explain to him how I scrubbed the tub out with cleanser afterward, he still acts like I have broken a major commandment. I think some of the Ultra-Religious are like that.

Bringing the now clean, pure white dog over to her, I hand the leash to the young woman. I bend down and whisper in Fluffy's ear, "This is your job. You gotta take care of her and all her babies." They take their young protector and leave for a new life on a lonely hilltop of Israel, just another two idealistic Hilltop Youth doing what they can. I turn and go back inside.

* * *

Hardly anything out of the ordinary happens during my last months. But then again, nothing is ordinary that happens in Israel.

My feet hit the metal mesh stairs leading up to the airliner. With each boot step, my mind screams "No!" but my body carries me on the journey home, my psyche a colorful swirl of emotions.

Did I help? What happened here? Mostly I wonder . . .

Did I do enough?

Chapter 18
The Rest of 2003
May Their Memories Be For A Blessing

May 5, 2003 - Gideon Lichterman, 27, of Ahiya, is killed and two other passengers, his six-year-old daughter Moriah and a reserve soldier, are seriously wounded when terrorists fire shots at their vehicle near Shvut Rachel, in Samaria. The Fatah al-Aqsa Martyrs' Brigades claim responsibility for the attack.

May 11, 2003 - Zion David, 53, of Givat Ze'ev near Jerusalem, is shot in the head and killed by Palestinian terrorists in a roadside ambush half a kilometer from Ofra, north of Jerusalem. Both Fatah and the Popular Front for the Liberation of Palestine claim responsibility for the attack.

May 17, 2003 - Gadi Levy and his wife Dina, aged 31 and 37, of Kiryat Arba are killed by a suicide bomber in Hebron. Hamas claims responsibility for the attack.

May 18, 2003 - Seven people are killed and 20 wounded in a suicide bombing on Egged bus no. 6 near French Hill in Jerusalem. Hamas claims responsibility for the attack. The victims: Olga Brenner, 52; Yitzhak Moyal, 64; Nelly Perov, 55; Marina Tsahivershvili, 44; Shimon Ustinsky, 68; and Roni Yisraeli, 34 - all of the Pisgat Ze'ev neighborhood in Jerusalem; and Ghalab Tawil, 42, of Shuafat. A second suicide bomber detonates his bomb when intercepted by police in northern Jerusalem. The terrorist is killed; no one else is injured.

May 19, 2003 - Kiryl Shremko, 22, of Afula; Hassan Ismail Tawatha, 41, of Jisr a-Zarqa; and Avi Zerihan, 36, of Beit Shean are killed and about 70 people are wounded in a suicide bombing at the entrance to the Amakim Mall in Afula. The Islamic Jihad and the Fatah al-Aqsa Martyrs Brigades both claim responsibility for the attack.

June 5, 2003 - The bodies of David Shambik, 26, and Moran Menachem, 17, both of Jerusalem, are found near Hadassah Ein Karem Hospital in Jerusalem, brutally beaten and stabbed to death.

June 8, 2003 - Sargent Major (Reserves) Assaf Abergil, 23, of Eilat; Sargent Major (Reserves) Udi Eilat, 38, of Eilat; Sergeant Major Boaz Emete, 24, of Beit She'an; and Sergeant Major (Reserves) Chen Engel, 32, of Ramat Gan are killed and four other reserve soldiers are wounded when Palestinian terrorists wearing IDF uniforms open fire on an IDF outpost near the Erez checkpoint and industrial zone in the Gaza Strip. Three terrorists are killed by IDF soldiers. The Fatah Al-Aqsa

Martyrs Brigades, Hamas and the Islamic Jihad issue a joint statement claiming responsibility for the attack.

June 8, 2003 - Staff-Sergeant Matan Gadri, 21, of Moshav Moledet is killed in Hebron while pursuing two Palestinian gunmen who earlier had wounded a Border Policeman on guard at the Tomb of the Patriarchs. The two terrorists are killed.

June 11, 2003 - Seventeen people are killed and over 100 wounded in a suicide bombing on Egged bus #14A outside the Klal building on Jaffa Road in the center of Jerusalem. Hamas claims responsibility for the attack. The victims: Sergeant Tamar Ben-Eliahu, 20, of Moshav Paran; Alan Beer, 47, of Jerusalem; Eugenia Berman, 50, of Jerusalem; Elsa Cohen, 70, of Jerusalem; Zvi Cohen, 39, of Jerusalem; Roi Eliraz, 22, of Mevaseret Zion; Alexander Kazaris, 77, of Jerusalem; Yaffa Mualem, 65, of Jerusalem; Yaniv Obayed, 22, of Herzliya; Bat-El Ohana, 21, of Kiryat Ata; Anna Orgal, 55, of Jerusalem; Zippora Pesahovitch;, 54, of Zur Hadassah; Bianca Shahrur, 62, of Jerusalem; Malka Sultan, 67, of Jerusalem; Bertine Tita, 75, of Jerusalem. Miriam Levy, 74, of Jerusalem died of her wounds on June 12. The 17th victim, male, who has not yet been positively identified, is believed to be a foreign worker from Eritrea.

June 12, 2003 - Avner Maimon, 51, of Netanya, is found shot to death in his car near Yabed in northern Samaria. The Fatah al-Aqsa Martyrs Brigades claims responsibility for the attack.

June 13, 2003 - Staff-Sergeant Mordechai Sayada, 22, of Tirat Carmel, is shot to death in Jenin by a Palestinian sniper as his Jeep patrol passed by. The Fatah al-Aqsa Martyrs Brigades claims responsibility for the attack.

June 17, 2003 - Noam Leibowitz, 7, of Yemin Orde is killed and three members of her family wounded in a shooting attack near the Kibbutz Eyal junction on the Trans-Israel Highway. The terrorist fired from the outskirts of the West Bank city of Kalkilya. The Fatah al-Aqsa Martyrs Brigades and the Popular Front for the Liberation of Palestine - General Command claim responsibility for the attack.

June 19, 2003 - Avner Mordechai, 58, of Moshav Sde Trumot, is killed when a suicide bomber blows up in his grocery on Sde Trumot, south of Beit Shean. The suicide bomber is killed. The Islamic Jihad claims responsibility for the attack.

June 20, 2003 - Zvi Goldstein, 47, of Eli, is killed when his car is fired upon in an ambush by Palestinian terrorists near Ofra, north of Ramallah. His parents, Eugene and Lorraine Goldstein, from New York, are seriously wounded and his wife lightly injured. Hamas claims responsibility for the attack.

June 26, 2003 - Amos (Amit) Mantin, 31, of Hadera, a Bezeq employee, is killed in a shooting attack in the Israeli Arab town of Baka al-Garbiyeh. The shots are fired by a Palestinian teenager, who is apprehended by police. The Fatah al-Aqsa Martyrs Brigades claims responsibility for the attack.

June 27, 2003 - Sergeant Major Erez Ashkenazi, 21, of Kibbutz Reshafim, an Israeli navy commando, is killed in an operation in Gaza to capture a Hamas cell, believed responsible for several bombings and the firing of anti-tank missiles in the Netzarim area.

June 30, 2003 - Krastyu Radkov, 46, a construction worker from Bulgaria, is killed in a shooting attack on the Yabed bypass road in northern Samaria, west of Jenin, while driving a truck. The Fatah Al-Aqsa Martyrs Brigades claims responsibility for the attack, in opposition to the declared ceasefire.

July 7, 2003 - Mazal Afari, 65, of Moshav K'far Yavetz is killed in her home on Monday evening and three of her grandchildren lightly wounded in a terrorist suicide bombing. The remains of the bomber are also found in the wreckage of the house. The Islamic Jihad claims responsibility for the attack.

July 15, 2003 - Amir Simhon, 24, of Bat Yam is killed when a Palestinian armed with a long-bladed knife stabbed passersby on Tel Aviv's beachfront promenade, after a security guard prevented him from entering the Tarabin cafe and is wounded. The terrorist, who is shot and apprehended, is a member of the Fatah Al-Aqsa Martyrs Brigades.

July 21, 2003 - The body of IDF soldier Corporal Oleg Shaichat, 20, of Upper Nazareth, abducted and murdered on July 21 while on his way home, is found on

July 28, buried in an olive grove near Kafr Kana, an Arab village in the Lower Galilee.

Aug 8, 2003 - Third Petty Officer Roi Oren, 20, an Israel Navy commando, is shot in the head and killed in an assault on a Hamas bomb factory in Nablus.

Aug 10, 2003 - Haviv Dadon, 16, of Shlomi, is struck in the chest and killed by shrapnel from an anti-aircraft shell fired by Hizbullah terrorists in Lebanon, as he sat with friends after work. Four others are wounded.

Aug 12, 2003 - Yehezkel (Hezi) Yekutieli, 43, of Rosh Ha'ayin, is murdered by a teenaged Palestinian suicide bomber who detonates himself as Yekutieli is shopping for his children's breakfast at his local supermarket.

Aug 12, 2003 - Erez Hershkovitz, 18, of Eilon Moreh, is murdered by a teenaged Palestinian suicide bomber who detonates himself at a bus stop outside Ariel less than half an hour after the Rosh Ha'ayin attack. Amatzia Nisanevitch, 22, of Nofim, dies of his wounds on August 28.

Aug 19, 2003 - Twenty-three people are murdered and 134 wounded when a Palestinian suicide bomber detonates himself on a No. 2 Egged bus in Jerusalem's Shmuel Hanavi neighborhood. Hamas claims responsibility for the attack. The victims: Avraham Bar-Or, 12, of Jerusalem; Binyamin Bergman, 15, of Jerusalem; Yaakov Binder, 50, of Jerusalem; Feiga Dushinski, 50, of Jerusalem; Miriam Eisenstein, 20, of Bnei Brak; Lilach Kardi, 22, of Jerusalem; Menachem Leibel, 24, of Jerusalem; Elisheva Meshulami, 16, of Bnei Brak;

Tehilla Nathanson, 3, of Zichron Ya'acov; Chava Nechama Rechnitzer, 19, of Bnei Brak; Mordechai Reinitz, 49, and Issachar Reinitz, 9, of Netanya; Maria Antonia Reslas, 39, of the Philippines; Liba Schwartz, 54, of Jerusalem; Hanoch Segal, 65, of Bnei Brak; Goldie Taubenfeld, 43, and Shmuel Taubenfeld, 3 months, of New Square, New York; Rabbi Eliezer Weisfish, 42, of Jerusalem; Shmuel Wilner, 50, of Jerusalem; Shmuel Zargari, 11 months, of Jerusalem. Fruma Rahel Weitz, 73, of Jerusalem dies of her wounds on August 23; Mordechai Laufer, 27, dies of his on September 5; and Tova Lev, 37, dies on September 12.

Aug 29, 2003 - Shalom Har-Melekh, 25, of Homesh is killed in a shooting attack while driving northeast of Ramallah. His wife, Limor, who is seven months pregnant, sustaines moderate injuries, and gives birth to a baby girl by Caesarean section. The Fatah al-Aqsa Brigades claims responsibility for the attack.

Sept 4, 2003 - Staff-Sergeant Gabriel Uziel, 20, of Givat Ze'ev is shot and mortally wounded by a terrorist sniper in Jenin; he dies en route to the hospital. The Fatah al-Aqsa Martyrs Brigades and the Islamic Jihad claim responsibility for the attack.

Sept 5, 2003 - 2nd Petty Officer Ra'anan Komemi, 23, of Moshav Aminadav, from the Naval Commandos is killed in a clash with armed Palestinians in Nablus. A senior Hamas bomb-maker, believed to have orchestrated several fatal suicide bombings, is also killed in the clash. Four soldiers are wounded, one seriously.

Sept 9, 2003 - Eight IDF soldiers are killed and 32 people are wounded in a suicide bombing at a hitchhiking post for soldiers outside a main entrance to the Tzrifin army base and Assaf Harofeh Hospital. Hamas claims responsibility for the attack. The victims: Senior Warrant Officer Haim Alfasi, 39, of Haifa; Chief Warrant Officer Yaakov Ben-Shabbat, 39, of Pardes Hanna; Corporal Mazi Grego, 19, of Holon; Captain Yael Kfir, 21, of Ashkelon; Corporal Felix Nikolaichuk, 20, of Bat Yam; Sergeant Yonatan Peleg, 19, of Moshav Yanuv; Sergeant Efrat Schwartzman, 19, of Moshav Ganei Yehuda; and Corporal Prosper Twito, 20, of Upper Nazareth.

Sept 9, 2003 - Seven people are killed and over 50 wounded when a suicide bomber at Cafe Hillel on Emek Refaim St., the main thoroughfare of the German Colony neighborhood in Jerusalem. Hamas claims responsibility for the attack. The victims: Dr. David Appelbaum, 51, and his daughter Nava Appelbaum, 20, of Jerusalem; David Shimon Avizadris, 51, of Mevaseret Zion; Shafik Kerem, 27, of Beit Hanina; Alon Mizrahi, 22, of Jerusalem; Gila Moshe, 40, of Jerusalem; and Yehiel (Emil) Tubol, 52, of Jerusalem.

Sept 25, 2003 - Staff-Sergeant Avihu Keinan, 22, of Shilo is killed and six soldiers wounded in an IDF operation to arrest wanted Islamic Jihad and Hamas terrorists in the El Boureij refugee camp in the southern Gaza Strip.

Sept 26, 2003 - Eyal Yeberbaum, 27, and seven-month-old Shaked Avraham, both of Negohot, south of Hebron, are killed during the holiday meal on the eve of Rosh Hashana in the Yeberbaum home when a Palestinian terrorist who infiltrated the settlement opens fire with an M-16 assault rifle. The terrorist is killed by IDF forces. The Islamic Jihad claims responsibility for the attack.

Oct 4, 2003 - Twenty-one people are killed, including four children, and 58 wounded in a suicide bombing carried out by a female terrorist from Jenin in the Maxim restaurant in Haifa. The Islamic Jihad claims responsibility for the attack. The victims: Admiral (Reserves) Ze'ev Almog, 71, of Haifa, and his wife Ruth Almog, 70; their son Moshe Almog, 43, and grandsons Tomer Almog, 9, and Assaf Staier, 11, all of Haifa; Zvi Bahat, 35, of Haifa; Mark Biano, 29, of Haifa, and his wife Naomi Biano, 25; Hana Francis, 39, of Fassouta; Mutanus Karkabi, 31, of Haifa; Sharbal Matar, 23, of Fassouta; Osama Najar, 28, of Haifa, cook; Nir Regev, 25, of Nahariya; Irena Sofrin, 38, of Kiryat Bialik; Bruria Zer-Aviv, 59, her son Bezalel Zer-Aviv, 30, and his wife Keren Zer-Aviv, 29, with their children Liran, 4, and Noya, 1, all of Kibbutz Yagur. Lydia Zilberstein, 58, dies on October 10 and George Matar, 57, dies October 15.

Oct 15, 2003 - Three American diplomatic personnel - John Eric Branchizio, 37, of Texas, John Martin Linde, Jr., 30, of Missouri, and Mark T. Parson, 31, of New York, are killed and one is wounded at the Beit Hanoun junction in the Gaza Strip when a massive bomb demolishes an armor-plated Jeep in a convoy carrying U.S. diplomats.

Oct 19, 2003 - Staff-Sergeant Erez Idan, 19, of Rishon Lezion, Sergeant Elad Pollack, 19, of Kiryat Motzkin, and Sergeant Roi Ya'acov Solomon, 21, of Tel Aviv, are killed and another soldier is seriously wounded while on patrol in Ein Yabrud, north of Ramallah, when terrorists fire on them from behind. The Fatah al-Aqsa Martyrs Brigades claims responsibility for the attack.

Oct 24, 2003 - Three IDF soldiers - Staff-Sergeant Alon Avrahami, 21, of Or Yehuda, Sergeant Adi Osman, 19, of K'far Sava, and Sergeant Sarit Schneor-Senior, 19, of Shoham - are killed and two others wounded when a Palestinian terrorist infiltrates the army base in the Gaza Strip settlement of Netzarim and opens fire on the soldiers' barracks. Hamas and the Islamic Jihad claim joint responsibility for the attack.

Nov 18, 2003 - Two IDF soldiers, Sergeant-Major Shlomi Belsky, 23, of Haifa, and Staff-Sergeant Shaul Lahav, 20, of Kibbutz Shomrat, are killed by a Palestinian terrorist who opens fire with an AK-47 assault rifle, hidden in a prayer rug, at a checkpoint on the tunnel bypass road, linking Jerusalem and the Gush Etzion bloc. The Fatah al-Aqsa Martyrs Brigades claims responsibility for the attack.

Nov 19, 2003 - Patricia Ter´n Navarrete, 33, of Ecuador is killed and four other tourists, pilgrims from Ecuador, are wounded when a terrorist enters the Israel-Jordan border crossing terminal north of Eilat from the Jordanian side and opens fire. The terrorist is killed by Israeli security guards.

Nov 22, 2003 - Two Israeli security guards, Ilya Reiger, 58, of Jerusalem, and Samer Fathi Afan, 25, of the Bedouin village Uzeir near Nazareth, are shot dead at a construction site along the route of the security fence near Abu Dis in East Jerusalem. The Jenin Martyrs' Brigades, affiliated with Fatah, claims responsibility for the attack.

Dec 22, 2003 - Captain Hagai Bibi, 24, of Maaleh Adumim, and Lieutenant Leonardo (Alex) Weissman, 23, of Afula are killed when a Palestinian terrorist opens fire and throws hand grenades as they emerged from their Jeep on the Kissufim-Gush Katif road in the Gaza Strip. The Fatah al-Aqsa Martyrs Brigades claims responsibility for the attack.

Dec 25, 2003 - Adva Fisher, 20, of K'far Sava; Staff-Sergeant Noam Leibowitz, 22, of Elkana; Corporal Angelina Shcherov, 19, of K'far Sava; and Corporal Rotem Weinberger, 19, of K'far Sava are killed and over 20 people are wounded in a suicide bombing at a bus stop at the Geha Junction, east of Tel Aviv, near Petah Tikva. The Popular Front for the Liberation of Palestine claims responsibility for the attack.[4]

---

[4] All the listings of terrorist attacks at the beginning of each chapter and here in Chapter 18 are from statistics on the website:
www.jewishvirtuallibrary.org

GLOSSARY:

Achshav — Stop (what I think it means).

Adonai — A name of G-d, which is not usually written, and only said in blessings.

Ahmed Jibril's Popular Front — A terrorist organization.

Aliyah — Literally to "go up," to move back to Israel.

Al-Qaeda — A terrorist organization.

Bal Tashuva — A returning Jew, who was lost to Jewish Nation and has decided to make amends and observe all mitzvahs and commandments.

Bar Mitzvah — When a boy is considered a man, around 12 or 13, he learns to read the week's parsha and usually gives a lecture. He is officially welcomed into the tribe as a full adult member, often followed by a party.

Baruch HaShem — Blessed be the Name (G-d).

Bat Mitzvah — When a girl is considered a woman. It is increasingly popular to treat the girls

	similar to the boys and have a party. Conservative and Reform allow girls to read the Parsha, just like the boys do. The Orthodox do not allow it.
BDU	Battle Dress Uniform.
Benching	Prayers of thanksgiving, done after meals.
BeShalach	A specific biblical verse reading of the week (parsha). Exodus 13:17-17:14 and the haftorah, Judges 4:4-5:31, includes the story of Devorah.
Bnei Noach	Sons & daughters of Noah, who is considered to be the person whom everyone is descended. A growing movement where Gentiles no longer feel comfortable with Christianity, yet are not willing to convert to Judaism. They follow the old testament, and the Seven laws of Noah.
Call Out	To be "called" for a tracking mission i.e. finding a lost child, missing person, Alzheimer's person etc.
Chabad	An Orthodox branch of Judaism which follows Rabbi Mendelssohn, and has emphasis on outreach.

Challah	Special braided bread used for the Sabbath. Also what a bride is called.
Charge(a gun)	Rack a gun.
Chas v'shalom	Heaven forbid.
China Central	Wal-Mart.
Diaspora	Jews outside of Israel.
Erev Rav	Mixed Multitude. When Moses led the Jews out of Egypt, many non-Jews joined in the slave rebellion and made their escape by pretending to be Jewish.
Fatah Al-Aqsa Brigades	A terrorist organization.
Fatah Al-Aqsa Martyrs' Brigades	A terrorist organization.
Fatah Tanzim	A terrorist organization.
G-d	Many religious Jews consider the use of the word "God" as breaking the commandment to not take G-d's name in vain, so they write it this way.
Gedud	Guard.

Gedud Ha'iveri	Jewish Guard.
Golani	A division of the IDF.
Ha'iveri	Jewish.
Halacha	The official rules regarding all things Jewish, mostly derives from Maimonides but added to by each generation's sages.
Hamas	A terrorist organization.
Hashem	Literally means "the name". A way of writing G-d's name so that one does not take G-d's name in vain.
Hidden Jew	Biblical prophecy states that when the Moshiach arrives, there will be many hidden Jews. Only the Moshiach will be able to tell who they are. Often a result of either pretending to be the dominant religion of a nation to avoid persecution, or intermarriage of a female Jew who subsequently takes her Gentile husband's name and religion. Her children are still halachically Jewish even though they may not know it or accept it.
IDF	Israel Defense Forces or Tzhal.

Intifada	A formal declaration by Muslim clerics saying that they are at war with Israel, and hence it is not just acceptable, but rewarded spiritually to kill Jews. It is often also rewarded in this life by suicide bombers' families being paid a salary after having killed Jews.
Islamic Jihad	A terrorist organization.
K'far	Village
K'far Tapuach	Apple Village.
Kabbalah	The secret knowledge of the spiritual meanings of the Torah written by Rabbi Shimon Bar Yochai.
Kelev	Dog.
Ken	Yes.
Ketuvim	Psalms, Book of Proverbs, Book of Job, Song of Solomon, Ruth, Lamentations, Ecclesiastes, Book of Esther, Daniel, Ezra, Nehemiah, Chronicles.
Klezmer	A style of Jewish music originating in Eastern Europe/Russia.
Lashon hora	Evil tongue or gossip. It is forbidden to gossip about a person.

LAX	Los Angeles International Airport.
Lo	No.
Marry Out	To marry outside of the Jewish faith.
Mezuzah	A passage of Torah inscribed on a sheet of parchment made from a kosher animal hide. Jewish people are required to place a mezuzah on the right side of every door frame of their dwelling places.
Migdol Mayim	Water tower.
Mikveh	A ritual bath used by religious Jewish women seven days after menses and seven to fourteen days after childbirth, as pre-scribed in Leviticus. Also used for purification.
Minyan	Ten Jewish men praying together.
Mitzvah	A good deed that is G-d ordained. Things like: be kind to widows and orphans, or to visit the elderly and sick. These are not just any good deed, but 613 specific codified deeds that G-d demands of Jews.

Moshiach	The Messiah.
NASAR	National Association of Search and Rescue.
Nevi'im	The Prophets. Includes the books of Isaiah, Jeremiah, Ezekiel, Kings, Hosea, Joel, Amos, Obadiah, Jonah, Micah, Haggai, Malachi, Nahum, Habakkuk, Zephaniah, and Zechariah.
Old Testament	The Original Testament of the Bible which includes the Torah, Nevi'im and Ketuvah.
Pareo	A piece of bright colored flower-printed fabric about two-yards long, that is wrapped around the waist to form a skirt, or over the bust to make a dress. Both men and women in the Hawaiian islands wear these.
Parsha	The official week's Torah reading that is the same for every Jew in every country.
Pesach	Passover.
Peyos	Side locks of hair that religious Jewish men wear.

PFLP	A terrorist organization. Popular Front for the Liberation of Palestine.
PMS	Pre-menstrual syndrome. Often used to describe an extra crabby or emotional woman.
Polydine	Similar to Betadine, an iodine solution.
PTSD	Post-Traumatic Stress Disorder.
Rebetizin	The wife of a Rabbi.
SAR	Search and Rescue.
Sar El	A volunteer organization that works under close supervision of Israel's Army and does helpful work for the Army.
Sefardi	Jews who originate from the Mediterranean areas.
Seven Laws of Noah	1. The prohibition of idolatry. 2. The prohibition of murder. 3. The prohibition of theft. 4. The prohibition of sexual immorality. 5. The prohibition of blasphemy. 6. The prohibition of eating flesh taken from an animal while it is still alive.

	7. The requirement of maintaining courts to provide legal recourse.
Shabbat	Sabbath, which starts Friday evening at sundown and ends Saturday evening when two stars are viewed in the sky.
Shiska	Yiddish term for a female gentile, somewhat derogatory.
Shmira	Guard duty.
Shul	Synagogue, Temple, a place for Jewish worship.
Shwarma	Similar to a Greek gyro only in Israel shwarma is kosher. Spiced Lamb or beef on a vertical spit which is roasted continually until an order is placed. Then the chef cuts thin slices off the roasting meat and puts it in a pita with hummus, salads, eggplants, spices.
Siddur	Jewish prayer book.
Summit	For some reason, in Hebrew, summit means the base of the hill, NOT the top of the hill like English. Possibly from the Hebrew word tzomet—sounds like summit in pronunciation, but means

crossroads.

Synagogue	Shul, Temple, a place for Jewish worship.
Tanakh	The Old or Original Testament of the Bible includes Torah, Nevi'im and Ketuvim.
Tapuach	Apple.
Tehillim	Psalms.
Temple	Usually called a Synagogue or Shul by Jews, because there is truly only one Temple. The "Temple" is located in Jerusalem on the Temple Mount, which is currently under the jurisdiction of the Waqf. The keys were given back to the Muslims in 1967 after the Temple Mount was won back to Jewish rule by heavy fighting in Jerusalem during the 1967 war. The non-religious Jews in government control in 1967 were afraid of world reaction, Muslim reaction, or other consequences of allowing religious Jewish control of the site of the first and second Jewish temples.

Torah	First five books of the Old Testament of the Bible. Given on Mt Sinai through Moses.
Transliteration	Hebrew and English have no common alphabet; therefore, a phonetic English pronunciation is imperative for the ease of use to English speakers.
Tremp	To hitchhike.
Tzitzit	Fringes on the corners of garments which religious Jews wear. Usually about 12" to 18" long and can have a single blue thread or be all white.
Ulpan	Hebrew language class.
USAR	Urban Search and Rescue.
West Bank	Israel's Biblical Heartland, called Judea and Samaria.
Yasomniks	Slang term for a division of police which is usually made up of large Russians who are known to ruthlessly use Billy clubs to crack skulls in order to quell riots.
Yeshiva	A Jewish school that studies Torah, Tanakh, Talmud, and the Jewish sages of history.

www.ingramcontent.com/pod-product-compliance
Lightning Source LLC
Chambersburg PA
CBHW021122300426
44113CB00006B/247